Early SPORTS Encyclopedias

BASEBALL AND SOFTBALL

by Brendan Flynn

Early Encyclopedias

An Imprint of Abdo Reference
abdobooks.com

abdobooks.com

Published by Abdo Reference, a division of ABDO, PO Box 398166, Minneapolis, Minnesota 55439. Copyright © 2024 by Abdo Consulting Group, Inc. International copyrights reserved in all countries. No part of this book may be reproduced in any form without written permission from the publisher. Early Encyclopedias™ is a trademark and logo of Abdo Reference.

052023
092023

THIS BOOK CONTAINS RECYCLED MATERIALS

Editor: Charlie Beattie
Series Designers: Candice Keimig, Joshua Olson

Library of Congress Control Number: 2022949129

Publisher's Cataloging-in-Publication Data

Names: Flynn, Brendan, author.
Title: Baseball and softball / by Brendan Flynn
Description: Minneapolis, Minnesota: Abdo Reference, 2024 | Series: Early sports encyclopedias | Includes online resources and index.
Identifiers: ISBN 9781098291259 (lib. bdg.) | ISBN 9781098277437 (ebook)
Subjects: LCSH: Baseball--Juvenile literature. | Softball--Juvenile literature. | Team sports--Juvenile literature. | Sports--History--Juvenile literature. | Encyclopedias and dictionaries--Juvenile literature.
Classification: DDC 796.03--dc23

CONTENTS

Introduction 4
    Overview 6
    Skills 18
    Positions 38
    Staying Safe 52
    All about Baseball 58
    All about Softball 76
    Top Baseball Teams 88
    Top Softball Teams 100
    Baseball Icons 108
    Softball Icons 120

Glossary 126
To Learn More 127
Index 127
Photo Credits 128

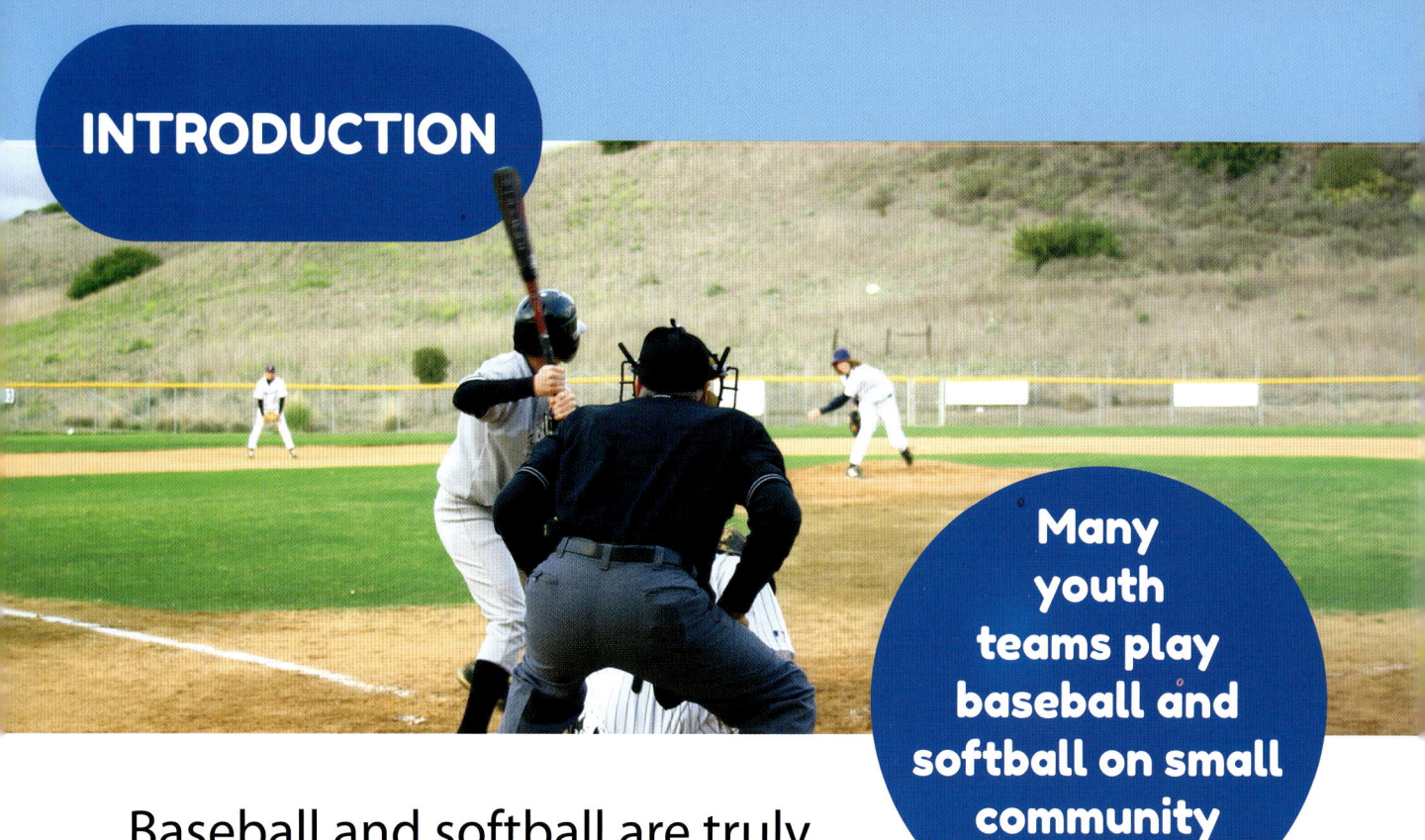

INTRODUCTION

Many youth teams play baseball and softball on small community fields.

Baseball and softball are truly American sports. Both were founded in the United States. The sports continue to be the most popular there. People of all ages and abilities can watch and play.

Baseball traces its roots to the mid-1800s. It's mostly played by boys and men. Today the best players compete in Major League Baseball (MLB). Each year, the winners of the American League (AL) and National League (NL) meet in the World Series.

Softball is like baseball, though players are mostly girls and women. The first softball game was played in 1887. Its rules have been updated through the years. Today the sport is most popular at the college level. Professional and international softball continue to grow, however.

Whether watching at a fancy ballpark or playing with friends at a park, baseball and softball are unique American traditions.

University of Oklahoma outfielder Jayda Coleman makes a great catch. Women's college softball is one of the fastest-growing sports in America.

OVERVIEW

Playing the Games

The rules of baseball and softball are mostly the same. Two teams play against each other. One team is in the field. The other team is batting. The fielding team has three outfielders and four infielders. It also has a pitcher in the middle of the infield. The catcher plays behind home plate.

A batter and catcher wait for a pitch.

A runner dives to try and beat a fielder to a base.

One player from the batting team stands at home plate. The play starts when the pitcher throws the ball toward the catcher. The batter tries to hit it. If the ball is hit, the batter runs to first base. The fielders try to catch the ball. The batter is out if the ball is caught in the air. If the ball hits the ground, a fielder can pick it up and throw it to first base. The batter is out if the throw beats them. If the batter reaches base before the ball, they are safe. A base runner can also be out if they are not touching a base and a fielder tags them with the ball.

OVERVIEW

A scoreboard keeps track of the score, the inning, the total number of outs, and the balls and strikes on the batter.

The batting team has three outs per inning. To score a run, one of its players must make it around the bases and touch home plate. Once three outs are made, the teams trade places. After three more outs, they trade places again. When both teams have had a chance to bat, it's called an inning. Most baseball games last nine innings. Softball games typically last seven innings.

Umpires enforce the rules. They decide whether runners are safe or out. They also call balls and strikes on pitches. Another job is to decide if a batted ball was in the field or in foul territory.

The home plate umpire crouches behind the catcher to get the best look at pitches.

OVERVIEW

A softball pitcher delivers the ball underhand.

Similar but Different

Softball and baseball are a lot alike. In both sports, there are nine players on each team. The four bases are laid out in the same diamond pattern. Batters try to hit the ball and run around the bases. Fielders try to catch the ball and get the batters out.

The biggest difference is how the ball is pitched. Softball pitchers throw underhand. Baseball pitchers, meanwhile, typically throw overhand. Softballs are also bigger than baseballs. However, baseball fields are bigger than softball fields.

Baseball players pitch by throwing the ball overhand.

OVERVIEW

The Field

Both baseball and softball infields are shaped like a diamond. There's a base at every corner. The pitcher's mound is in the middle.

The outfield is a large, grassy area beyond the infield. A fence forms the edge of the outfield. If the batter hits the ball over the fence, it's a home run.

White lines in the grass on both sides of the outfield mark fair territory. If a ball lands inside the lines, it's in play. If it lands outside the lines, it's a foul ball. Each team has a bench or a dugout. One is along the first-base line. The other is along the third-base line.

FUN FACT!

Baseball usually has a grass infield. A softball infield is made entirely of dirt.

outfield fence

outfield

second base

pitcher's mound*

left-field line

right-field line

third base

first base

dugout

dugout

home plate

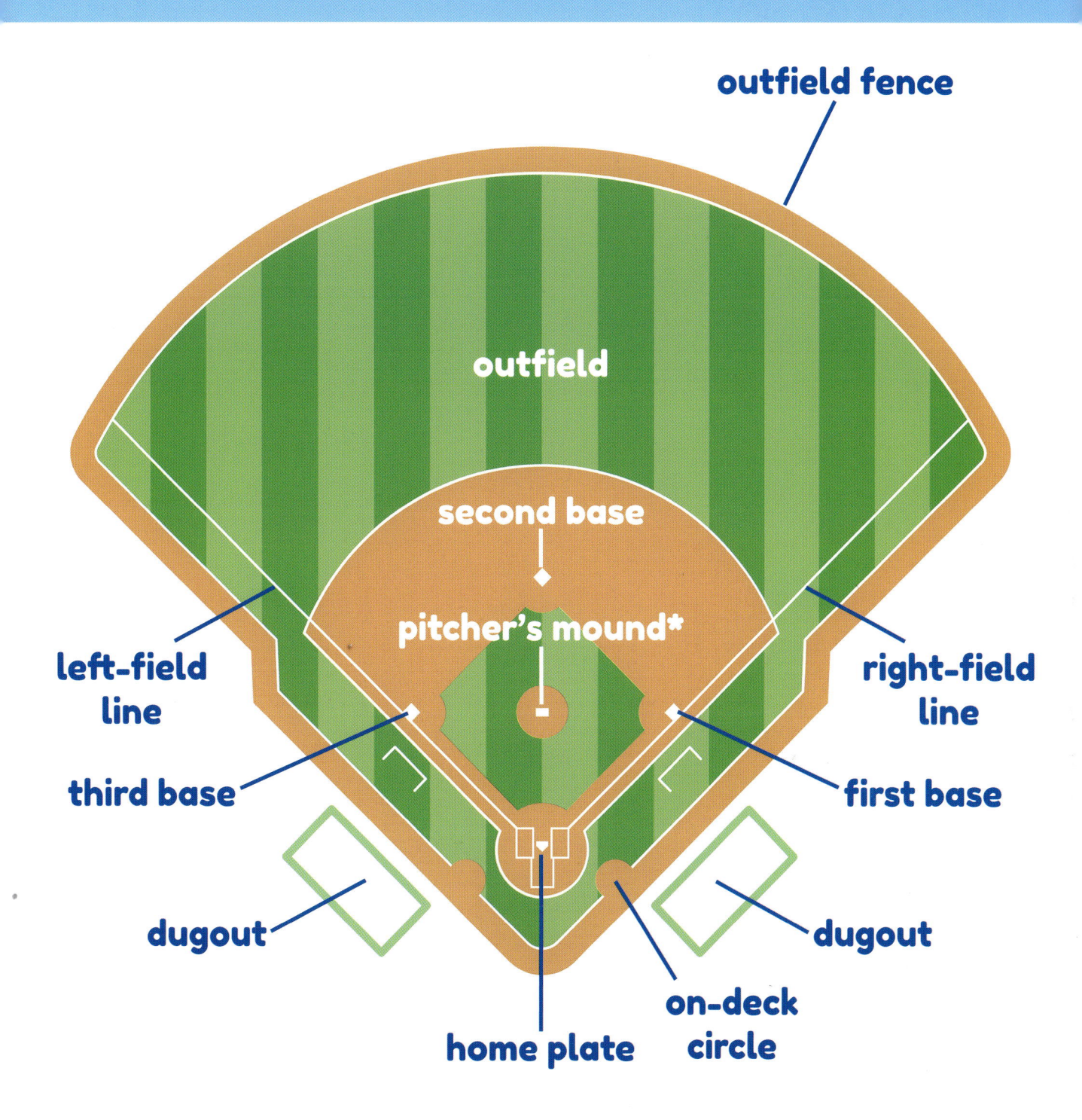

on-deck circle

* The pitcher's mound is raised in baseball but flat to the ground in softball.

OVERVIEW

Uniforms and Equipment

Players wear uniforms to show which team they play for. In baseball, uniforms include a cap, a jersey, pants, and socks. Softball players sometimes wear a visor rather than a cap. Players also wear shoes called cleats or spikes. These shoes grip the field as players move. Every player also wears a glove in the field.

Other basic equipment includes bats and balls. A bat can be made of carbon fiber or wood. Professional baseball leagues use wood bats.

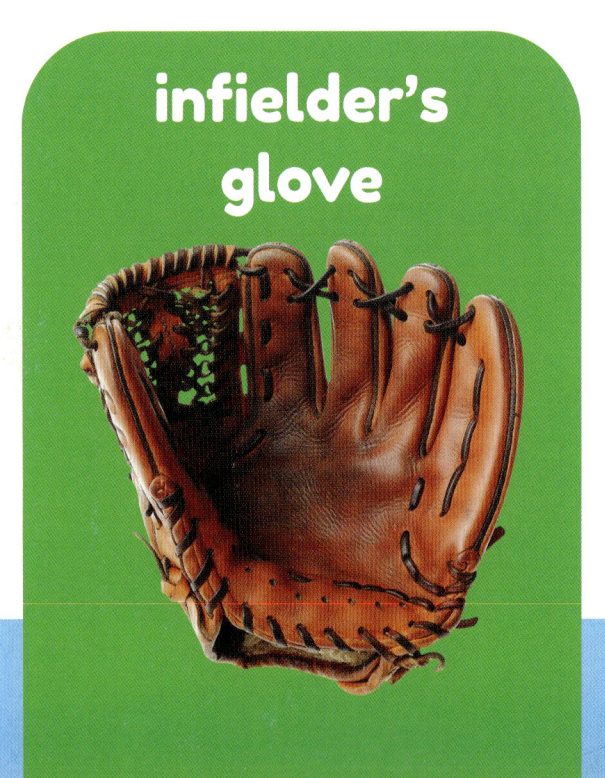

infielder's glove

first baseman's glove

Baseballs have white leather covers and red stitches to hold them together. Softballs have yellow leather and red stitches.

Every field needs three bases and a home plate. The bases are white squares. Home plate is flat and looks like a rectangle with a triangle attached.

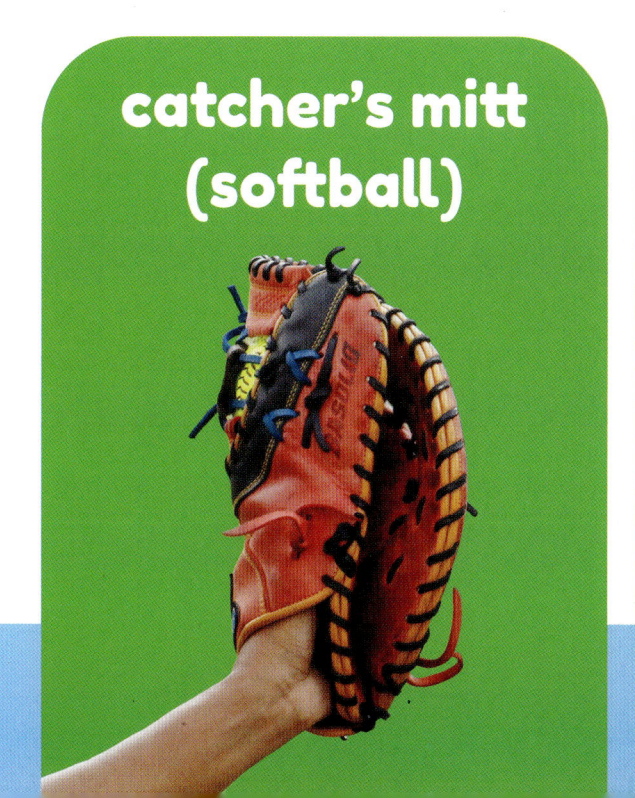

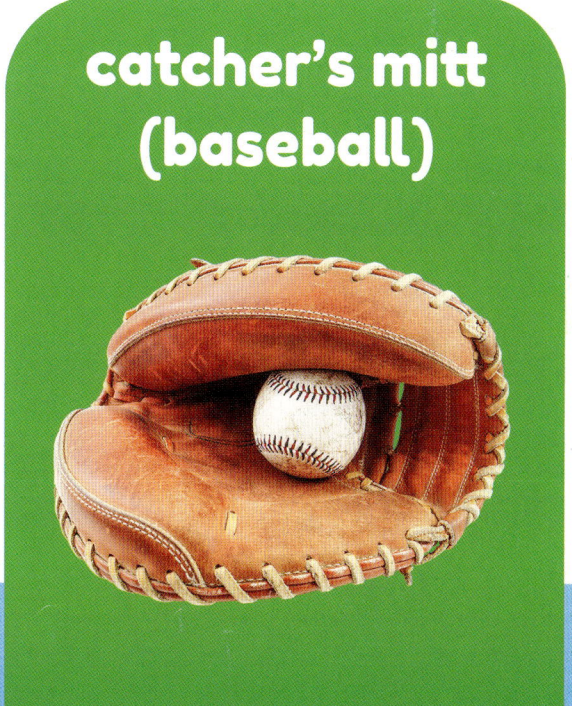

outfielder's glove

catcher's mitt (softball)

catcher's mitt (baseball)

OVERVIEW

The At-Bat

In both baseball and softball, every play starts with an at-bat. That's when a batter stands at home plate to face the pitcher. Each side of the plate has a batter's box.

A batter waits for a pitch during a softball game.

Batters are either left-handed or right-handed. Right-handed batters line up on the third-base side. They place the right hand above the left when holding the bat. Left-handed batters are the opposite. Switch-hitters are comfortable batting on either side of the plate.

Pitchers start each play on the mound. They push off a slab of rubber for extra traction and force. The goal is to get the batter out. A pitcher can do this by recording three strikes. Otherwise, pitchers try to make the batter hit into an out in the field.

The Strike Zone

The strike zone is an imaginary box. It goes from the batter's chest to his knees and is as wide as home plate.

SKILLS

Oakland Athletics pitcher Shintaro Fujinami hits the outside corner with a pitch.

Pitching

Control is very important for pitchers. The best pitchers are able to pitch to different spots in the strike zone. If a batter is good at hitting low pitches, the pitcher should adjust and throw high in the zone. The best pitchers hit the edges—or "corners"—of the plate. Those pitches are usually harder for batters to hit.

Baseball pitchers also need to keep runners from stealing bases. They do this by throwing the ball quickly to a base when the runner is taking a lead. That's called a pickoff move. Softball players cannot lead off until the ball leaves the pitcher's hand.

Cleveland pitcher Shane Bieber tries to pick off a runner at first base during a game in 2019.

SKILLS

Making Contact

The batter tries to put the ball in play by hitting it with her bat. If a fielder catches the ball in the air, the batter is out. But if the ball touches the ground and the batter reaches first base before a fielder throws the ball there, then it's a hit.

A hitter keeps her eye on the ball in an effort to make contact.

Crystl Bustos of Team USA connects on a home run during the 2008 Olympics in Beijing, China.

A hit can be a single, a double, a triple, or a home run. Singles, doubles, and triples depend on how many bases the batter takes while the fielders chase the ball. A home run is when a batter makes it around all four bases on one hit. The ball usually goes over the fence on a home run.

SKILLS

Fielding

Fielders each have a position where they start each play. The pitcher is on the mound. The catcher squats behind home plate. The first baseman and third baseman stand near their bases. The second baseman and shortstop cover the middle of the infield. Three players cover the outfield. One stands in left field, one in center field, and one in right field.

Any fielder can make an out by catching the ball before it hits the ground. Infielders often pick up ground balls and throw them to first base to get outs. Outfielders must be able to cover a large amount of space. They also race to track down hits and throw the ball back to the infield quickly.

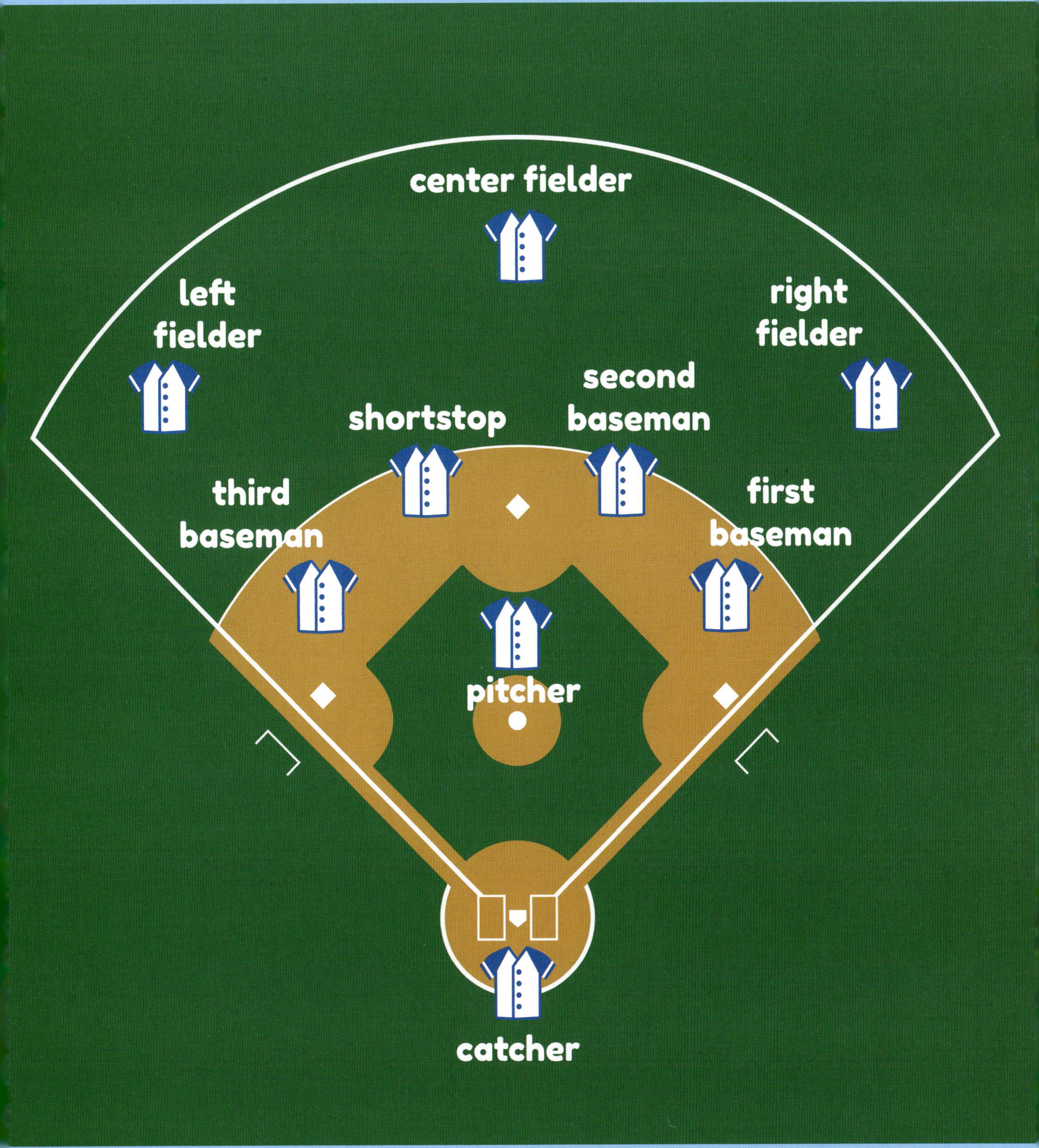
center fielder
left fielder
right fielder
second baseman
shortstop
third baseman
first baseman
pitcher
catcher

SKILLS

Kalei Harding of Florida State University runs out of the batters' box during a game in 2021.

Base Running

Batters who run hard right away have a better chance of reaching first base before a throw. They can also stretch hits to the outfield into doubles and triples.

Once on base, a runner can try to steal. That means he runs to the next base while the pitcher is throwing. Timing is key when trying to steal.

If a runner leaves early, the pitcher can stop his motion and pick the runner off. If a base stealer runs too late, it will be easier for the catcher to throw him out.

The best runners also get a good read on the ball when it's hit. They freeze on a line drive, in case an infielder catches it. On a long fly ball, they watch the outfielders to see if the ball will be caught. And they always run hard when there are two outs.

A baseball player takes off from first base.

SKILLS

Hitting Basics

No two batters are the same. Everyone stands and holds a bat differently when they are waiting for a pitch. Young hitters should try different ways to do both. Eventually they will find what feels comfortable.

Most good swings do look the same. Hitters first shift their weight toward the back foot. This is called the "load." They usually do this when the pitcher first starts the pitching motion. Then they step toward the pitcher with the front foot. That's called the "stride." They often

Each hitter has a unique batting stance.

A relaxed, smooth swing helps a hitter make contact.

put their toes down at the time when they decide whether to swing at the pitch. And if they swing, hitters keep their eyes on the ball. Young hitters should focus more on making contact. With good basics, power hitting will develop on its own.

Batting Average

A player's batting average is found by dividing his total number of hits by his number of at-bats. A .300 batting average is considered very good. This means on average the player gets a hit three times for every ten at-bats.

SKILLS

Trea Turner of the Los Angeles Dodgers connects on a bunt during a game in 2022.

Bunting

A bunt is when a batter gently taps the ball without swinging through. Usually the ball doesn't travel very far. This makes it difficult to field.

There are two types of bunts. A sacrifice bunt is used when the hitting team has runners on base they want to advance. The batter squares around with both feet facing the pitcher. The bat is held level over the plate and is used to tap the pitch down to the ground. The bunt should be aimed up one of the baselines.

A drag bunt is used by fast runners to try for a base hit. As the pitcher is delivering the ball, the batter moves his top hand up the bat handle. At the last second, he squares to bunt and taps the ball toward the ground.

Jose Altuve of the Houston Astros gets a running start on a drag bunt.

SKILLS

Softball Hitting

Many of the skills related to hitting a baseball are the same in softball. But because softball pitchers are closer to home plate, batters have less time to decide whether to swing. The batter needs to be focused on seeing the ball.

A hitter has less than one second to react to a pitch in softball.

A batter must keep both feet inside the batter's box while attempting a slap hit.

It helps to know if the pitcher has a good changeup and when she likes to throw it.

Another big difference in softball is the slap. It's a skill that many left-handed batters use to reach base. It's similar to a drag bunt, but the batter swings at the ball just as she starts to run.

SKILLS

Baseball Pitching Basics

Most baseball pitchers throw a few types of pitches. A fastball is a pitch that moves straight at top speed. A changeup looks like a fastball, but it's slower. Breaking balls are pitches that change directions on the way to the plate. A ball can be made to move in many different directions.

Breaking Balls
Young pitchers should focus on throwing fastballs and changeups. Throwing too many breaking balls at a young age can damage a pitcher's arm.

Pitchers can use a windup. That can help add power to the pitch. Or they can pitch from the stretch. That is a shorter type of windup to get the ball home more quickly. Doing so makes it harder for baserunners to steal.

It is important for pitchers to develop a consistent motion on the mound.

SKILLS

Softball Pitching Basics

In softball, pitchers don't throw from a mound. The pitcher's plate is on flat ground. Softball pitchers have to use their bodies to create momentum. That starts with the windup. Throwing a ball underhand as hard as possible isn't a natural skill for most people. Pitchers must perfect their windup.

University of Missouri pitcher Jordan Weber winds up during a 2021 game.

As with baseball pitching, control is important. Good softball pitchers try to hit the corners of the plate. But they also try to mix low and high pitches. One key pitch in softball is the rise ball. It is thrown with backspin. It looks like it is coming right over the plate. But as it gets to the hitter, it moves up. The goal is to get the batter to swing under it.

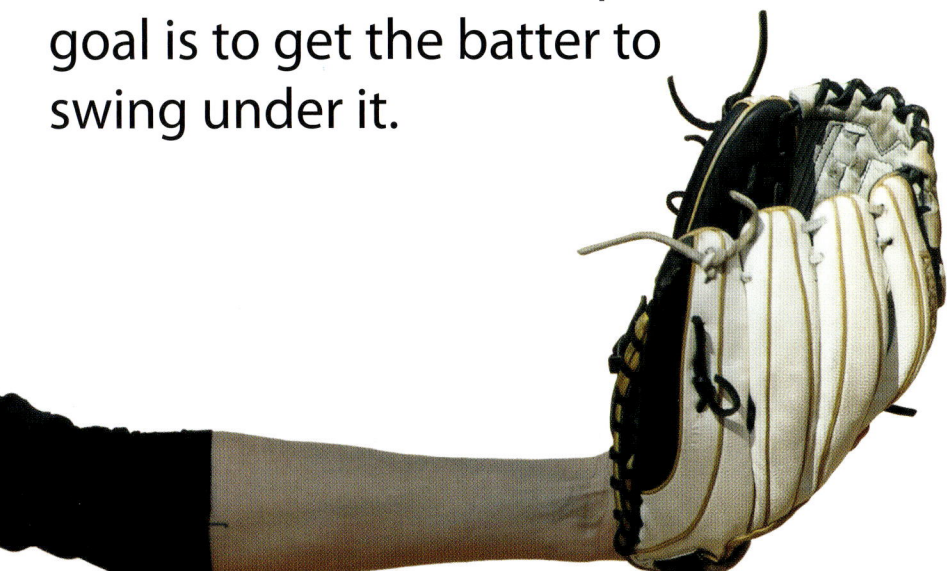

SKILLS

Staying alert is one of the keys to being a good fielder.

Mental Skills

Baseball and softball are sports with a lot of downtime. Players need to be able to stay focused on the game when in the field. One way to do that is to ask themselves questions. How many outs are there in the inning? What's the count on the batter? Where are the base runners? Where will I throw the ball if it comes my way?

Confidence is another big part of the mental game. It's especially important when batting. Hitters have to deal with a lot of failure. It's often said that the best hitters in the world only get three hits for every ten times at the plate. Good players trust themselves and don't panic when they aren't hitting well.

Even the best baseball and softball hitters go through tough stretches at the plate.

POSITIONS

Pitcher

Baseball and softball pitchers have an important role in the game. A good pitcher can dominate an opponent and give her own team a good

> A pitcher fields a ground ball and looks to throw to first base.

Philadelphia Phillies pitcher Zack Wheeler covers first base on a play against the New York Mets.

chance to win. But there's more to being a pitcher than throwing strikes. The best pitchers also field their position well.

After delivering the pitch, it's helpful to be in fielding position. A pitcher squares to home plate, ready to field a ball hit back to them.

On any ground ball to a pitcher's left, the pitcher should start running toward first base. If the first baseman goes to field the ball, she might need to throw it to the pitcher to get the out.

POSITIONS

A softball catcher gloves and holds a pitch during a college game in 2021.

Catcher

The catcher has many important jobs during a game. The first is to help the pitcher decide which pitch to throw. Catchers "call" the game by flashing signals to the pitcher with their fingers.

Electronic Signs

In 2022, MLB catchers started using transmitters in their armbands to call pitches. The device would relay the signal for the next pitch to a speaker in the pitcher's cap.

Catchers also receive pitches, of course. Sometimes they need to block low pitches that bounce. They do this by dropping to their knees and getting their arms and chests in front of the ball. Because of this, catchers need to be tough and durable.

Catchers must also be able to throw out runners trying to steal bases. To do this, a catcher needs a strong throwing arm. Catchers also need good reflexes to get out of a crouch and make a quick throw.

A catcher tries to throw out a base stealer.

POSITIONS

First Base

First basemen are often strong, powerful hitters. They are usually some of the tallest and biggest players on a team. That size can help on defense too. Having a big target at first base can help the other infielders aim their throws.

To catch those throws, first basemen have to be sure-handed. Sometimes the throws are low. The best first basemen are good at scooping low throws or even catching them on a hop.

Left-handed throwers have an advantage at first base.

New York Mets first baseman Daniel Murphy lunges to scoop a low throw.

A softball first baseman reaches for a high throw.

Because most of the field is to their right, they don't have to turn their bodies to make throws to other fielders.

POSITIONS

Philadelphia Phillies second baseman Jean Segura backhands a ball.

Second Base

Second basemen set up midway between first and second base. They're responsible for ground balls up the middle. They also might need to cover extra ground to their left so the first baseman can cover first base for a throw.

One of the most important jobs of a second baseman is turning double plays. When a runner is on first, second basemen run to second base every time a ground ball is hit to the shortstop or third baseman. Second basemen catch the throw with a foot on the base to get the first out. Then they need to avoid the sliding runner and make a strong throw to first. This play is called the "pivot."

University of Texas second baseman Janae Jefferson tries to turn a double play.

POSITIONS

Third Base

Like first basemen, third basemen are usually strong hitters. But they have an important role to play on defense as well. Third basemen need strong arms to make the long throw across the diamond. They also need great reflexes. A ball hit hard down the third-base line gets there quickly.

FUN FACT!

Every year, the best fielders at each position in MLB are given the Gold Glove Award. Former Baltimore Oriole Brooks Robinson won the award 16 times at third base.

University of Montana third baseman Kylie Becker sets up before a pitch.

Kansas City Royals third baseman Nate Eaton attempts to make a throw on the run.

    The best third basemen also are agile. One of the toughest plays is when third basemen charge in to field a slowly rolling ball. They have to pick up the ball, usually bare-handed. Then, in one motion, they need to make an accurate throw to first base. The best third basemen make that play look easy. But it requires a ton of skill.

POSITIONS

Shortstop

Shortstops play between second and third base. They are often the best athletes on the team. They need to be fast to cover ground to their left and right. They need strong arms to make long throws to first base. Finally, shortstops often serve as the "cutoff." That means they take long throws from outfielders and relay the ball to the right base.

Mexico shortstop Anissa Urtez makes a difficult throw during the 2021 Olympics in Tokyo, Japan.

Agility is important for a shortstop. On ground balls to the right side of the infield, shortstops cover second base. They also often cover second base on stolen base attempts. That means they have to race over from their positions, catch the throw, and tag the runner.

Leading the Way

Shortstops are considered the leaders of the infield. If they call for a ball, other infielders are supposed to get out of the way.

Colorado Rockies shortstop Trevor Story tries to tag out a runner from the Washington Nationals during a game in 2018.

POSITIONS

Outfielders are taught to use both hands to catch the ball.

Outfield

The left fielder, center fielder, and right fielder cover the outfield. Speed is important for outfielders. They track down long fly balls and catch them for outs. They also race to cut off hits before the ball rolls all the way to the fence. That can keep runners from advancing.

The right fielder needs the strongest arm because of the long throw from right field to third base. Outfielders need accurate arms as well. It's important for them to hit the cutoff. Center fielders have the most ground to cover. Like shortstops, they are in charge of the other outfielders. Any ball that a center fielder calls for is considered theirs.

An outfielder releases a long throw back toward the infield.

STAYING SAFE

Equipment

Safety equipment in baseball and softball has changed a lot over the years. Until the 1970s, MLB batters didn't even need to wear a helmet! But one position has always had extra protection. Catchers take a beating behind home plate.

A full set of catcher's gear starts with a helmet and mask. These days the mask is usually attached to the helmet. Most masks extend to the top of the chest. That helps protect the neck from foul balls.

A chest protector with shoulder pads covers the catcher's torso. Hard plastic leg guards cover the knees, shins, and tops of the feet. Recently, some catchers have been wearing pads known as "knee savers" behind their lower legs. They take some weight off the knees when crouching.

helmet

mask

chest protector

catcher's mitt

leg guards

STAYING SAFE

Softball Safety

The smaller field in softball creates some extra safety risks. The ball can fly off the bat at 70 miles per hour (113 kmh) or more. That doesn't give infielders much time to react. Youth players are required to wear masks in the field.

A softball player wears a facemask in the field.

A double-wide first base gives both the fielder and runner a safe place to step.

Softball batters also don't have much time to react to a pitch. If a fastball comes high and inside, it can be hard to get out of the way. Most softball hitters have masks that attach to their helmets to protect their faces from high pitches.

Many softball diamonds use a double-wide base at first base. That helps runners avoid stepping on the first baseman when they run through the base.

STAYING SAFE

MLB catcher Ivan Rodriguez catches a foul ball near the protective netting behind home plate.

Fan Safety

A day at the ballpark can be fun for the whole family. But fans should be ready for a ball to fly into the stands at any moment.

Ballparks have protected fans behind home plate for years. At lower levels, a chain-link fence known as a backstop keeps balls from hitting those fans. At larger ballparks, a net hangs in front of and above the fans behind home plate. But fans were still getting hurt by line drives that flew into the seats above the dugouts and down the lines.

In 2020, all MLB stadiums added extra netting. The protection for fans now extends from foul pole to foul pole in some stadiums.

Many fans bring their own gloves to the park in hopes of catching a ball in the stands.

ALL ABOUT BASEBALL

Baseball Origins

Baseball's most popular origin story was proven to be a myth. A US Army soldier named Abner Doubleday was said to have invented baseball in 1839 in Cooperstown, New York. However, similar sports were played in England as early as the 1700s.

After supposedly creating baseball, Abner Doubleday served as a general in the US Army.

Until the 1880s, many fielders played without gloves.

Organized baseball took a step forward in 1845. That's when the first set of rules for the game were published. They were called the Knickerbocker Rules. They were named for a team that was playing in New York City. Alexander Cartwright wrote the rules. They included the dimensions of the diamond. Other Knickerbocker Rules included three strikes for an out and three outs per inning. Because of this, many people say Cartwright created baseball.

ALL ABOUT BASEBALL

Early MLB Years

A few professional leagues were formed in the 1860s and early 1870s. But none of them lasted. Then, in 1876, the NL was created. Though the teams have changed, it's the same NL that is playing today.

In 1882 the American Association (AA) was formed. It was a rival to the NL. The AA lasted only ten years. Then a minor league called the

The 1869 Cincinnati Red Stockings were the first professional baseball team.

Ban Johnson helped form the AL in 1901. The new league led to the creation of the modern MLB.

Western League decided to make a change. It wanted to compete with the NL to sign the best players. The Western League changed its name to the AL in 1901. In 1903, the two leagues played the first World Series.

ALL ABOUT BASEBALL

Leroy "Satchel" Paige, *right,* shakes hands with David Barnhill before a Negro Leagues game at Yankee Stadium in 1942.

Negro Leagues

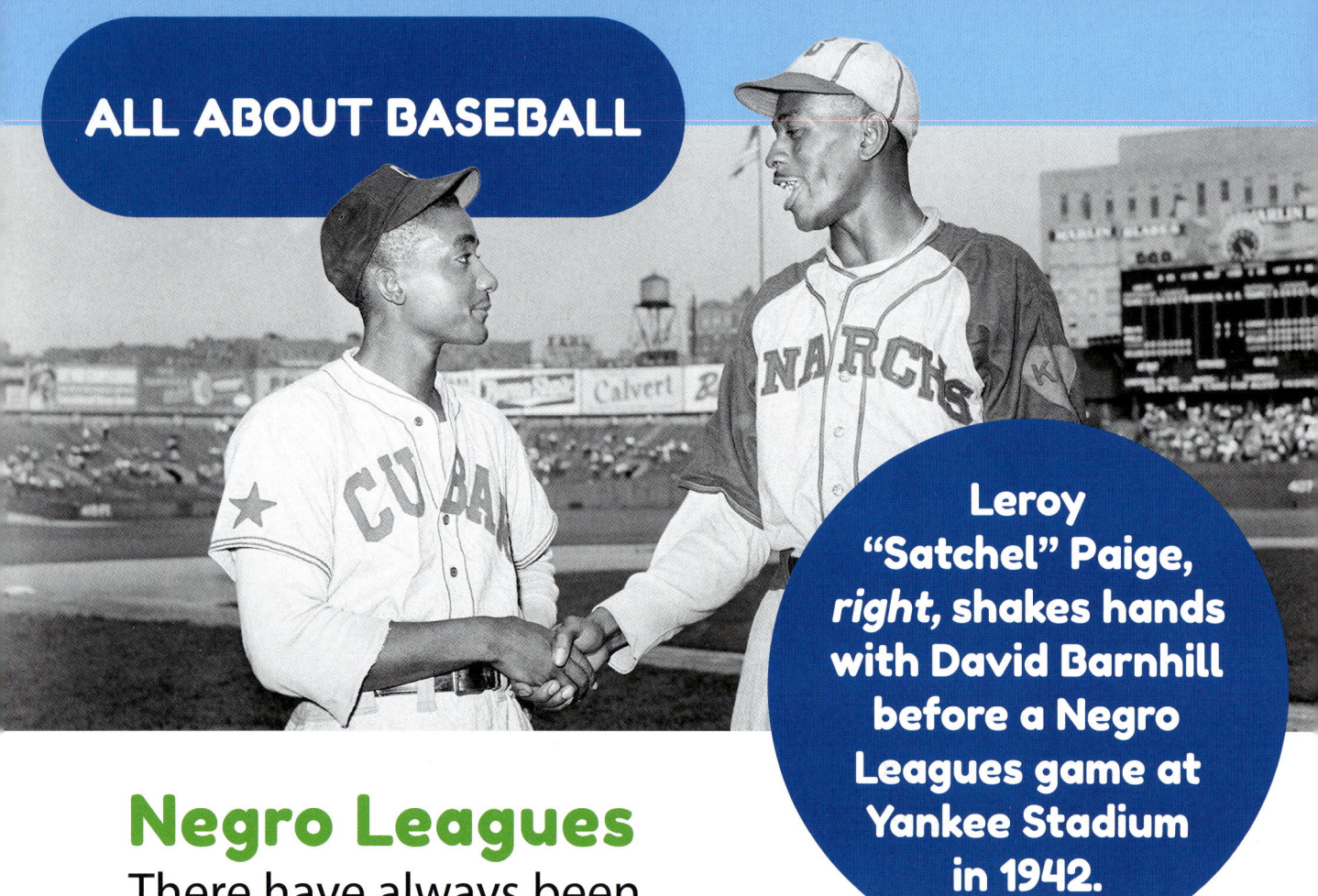

There have always been talented Black baseball players. However, a racist agreement among owners meant Black players couldn't participate in MLB for many years. It wasn't an official rule. But the owners agreed to not sign Black players.

The Black players created their own leagues. The most well-known was the Negro National League, formed in 1920. Many teams were in cities that also had MLB teams. They often played in the same stadiums. Legendary players such as Josh Gibson, Cool Papa Bell, and Satchel Paige starred in the Negro Leagues.

In 1947, Jackie Robinson was signed by the Brooklyn Dodgers of MLB. He became the first Black player to play in the league since the 1880s. Soon MLB teams rushed to desegregate their rosters. The Negro Leagues eventually shut down. But they are a huge part of baseball history.

James "Cool Papa" Bell was one of the fastest baseball players. He played 21 seasons in the Negro Leagues and was an All-Star eight times.

ALL ABOUT BASEBALL

MLB Growth

From 1903 to 1952, the same 16 teams played in the same cities in the AL and NL. Some cities had a team in each league. Then many teams started to move to cities that had no teams. For example, in 1954 the Philadelphia Athletics moved to Kansas City. Later they moved again to Oakland.

In the early days of MLB, the league had no teams west of St. Louis.

A huge crowd gathers to welcome the Dodgers to Los Angeles in April 1958.

The biggest moves came in 1958. Before then, no teams were located on the west coast. Then the owners of the Brooklyn Dodgers and the New York Giants moved their teams to California. MLB began to realize that many other cities could support teams. The leagues began expanding. New teams were soon added throughout the country. Two new teams even played in Canada. Today there are 30 MLB teams, 15 in each league.

ALL ABOUT BASEBALL

Third baseman José Ramírez of the Cleveland Guardians is one of many MLB stars from the Dominican Republic.

A Global Game

Baseball is popular in several countries around the world. Canada and Mexico have long histories with the game. Baseball also is wildly popular in many Latin American countries. Cuba, Venezuela, and the Dominican Republic all have rich baseball traditions. Japan, South Korea, and Australia also have strong professional leagues. Still, many of the top players from those countries leave to join MLB if they can.

Baseball is beginning to catch on in Europe. American soldiers shared the game with Italians and Germans during and after World War II (1939–45). However, the sport is still less popular in Europe than other sports such as soccer and basketball.

World Baseball Classic

The World Baseball Classic began in 2006. It draws the top professional players in the world to represent their home countries. Each tournament is made up of 20 international teams.

The Venezuelan Professional Baseball League starts its season each October.

ALL ABOUT BASEBALL

Little League to College

In 1938, a man named Carl Stotz put together a baseball program for kids in Williamsport, Pennsylvania. He adjusted the rules and the size of the field to fit younger players. The next year, Stotz founded Little League Baseball.

Today nearly 200,000 teams from more than 80 countries play Little League. They come together every August to play in the Little League World Series.

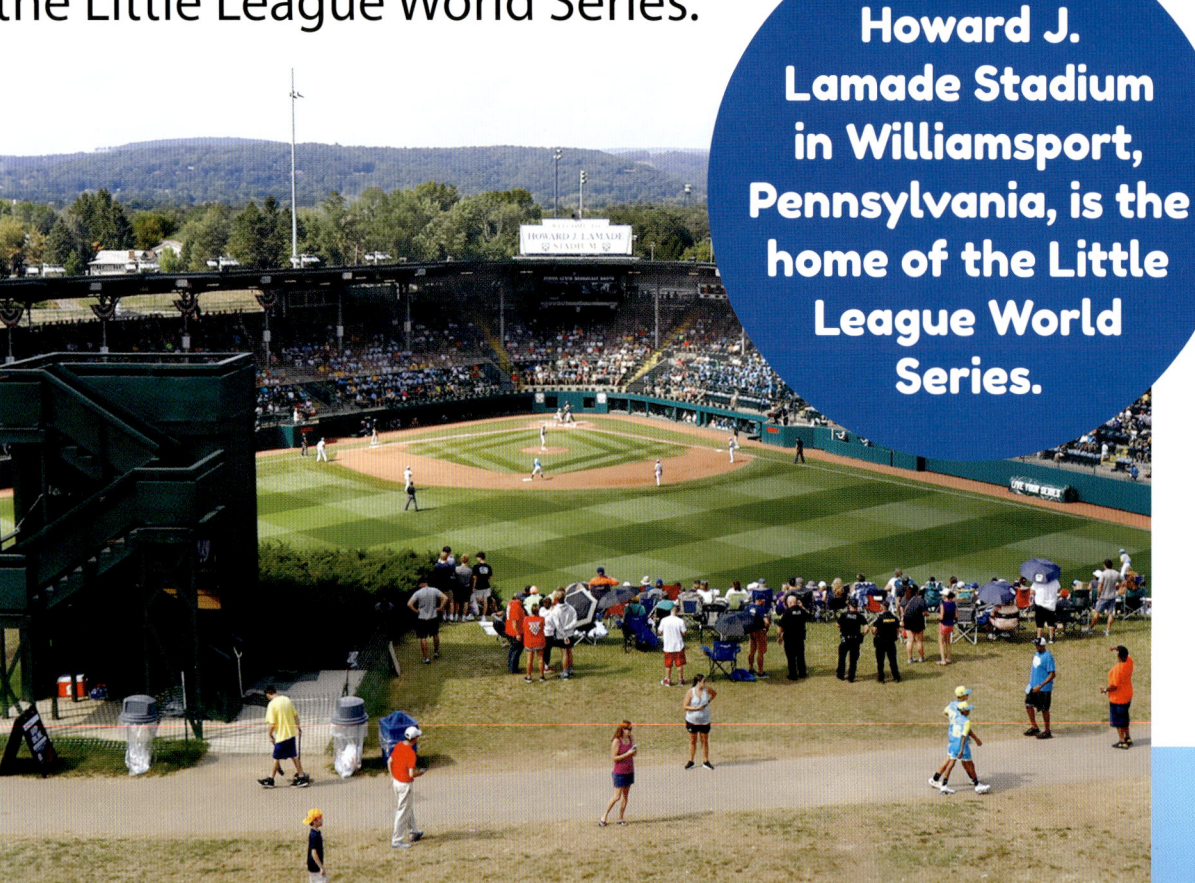

Howard J. Lamade Stadium in Williamsport, Pennsylvania, is the home of the Little League World Series.

Mississippi State University shortstop Lane Forsythe connects on a pitch during the 2021 College World Series in Omaha, Nebraska.

Aside from school teams, other leagues were formed for different age-groups. American Legion baseball is a popular summer activity for high school–aged players. Many of the best college players spend their summers playing in wood-bat leagues. That helps them prepare for pro ball, where metal bats are against the rules.

ALL ABOUT BASEBALL

Outfielder Wilyer Abreu bats for the Portland Sea Dogs in a 2022 game. The Sea Dogs are the Double-A team for the Boston Red Sox.

The Farm System

Each MLB team has its own minor league teams. They are often called the team's "farm system." Young players are sent to these teams to work on their skills before they become major leaguers.

The minor league system looks like a ladder. MLB is at the top of the ladder. One step below is Triple-A. Sometimes players go back and forth between Triple-A and their MLB team many times in the same season.

The other steps on the ladder are Double-A, High-A, Low-A, and Rookie League. Players drafted out of high school usually start at the Rookie level. College players often start at one of the Class A levels.

Minnesota Twins Farm System

ALL ABOUT BASEBALL

The Majors

MLB has 30 teams. Half of them play in the AL. The other half are in the NL. Each league is made up of three divisions. Each of those divisions has five teams.

Since 1962, MLB's teams have been scheduled for 162 games per season. In 2023, MLB changed its scheduling so that every team would play the other 29 teams at least once each season. At the end of the season, the teams with the best records make the playoffs. That includes all the division winners. The MLB playoffs have included six teams from each league since 2022.

Interleague Play

AL and NL teams used to play each other only in spring training and the World Series. MLB added interleague play in 1997. Now teams from different leagues play each other every year.

Map of MLB Teams

ALL ABOUT BASEBALL

The World Series

The MLB season ends in early October. Then the NL and AL have their own playoffs. The two teams that advance through the playoffs are crowned the league champions. And the AL and NL champs meet every year in the World Series.

Fans and players celebrate after the Houston Astros defeated the Philadelphia Phillies to win the 2022 World Series.

New York Yankees shortstop Derek Jeter celebrates a game-winning home run in Game 4 of the 2001 World Series.

The first World Series between the AL and NL champions was held in 1903. The Boston Americans (AL) beat the Pittsburgh Pirates (NL) five games to three. The next year, the New York Giants won the NL. Their manager, John McGraw, refused to play the AL champs from Boston. But starting in 1905, the World Series has been played every fall except one. In 1994, a players' strike canceled the season in August.

ALL ABOUT SOFTBALL

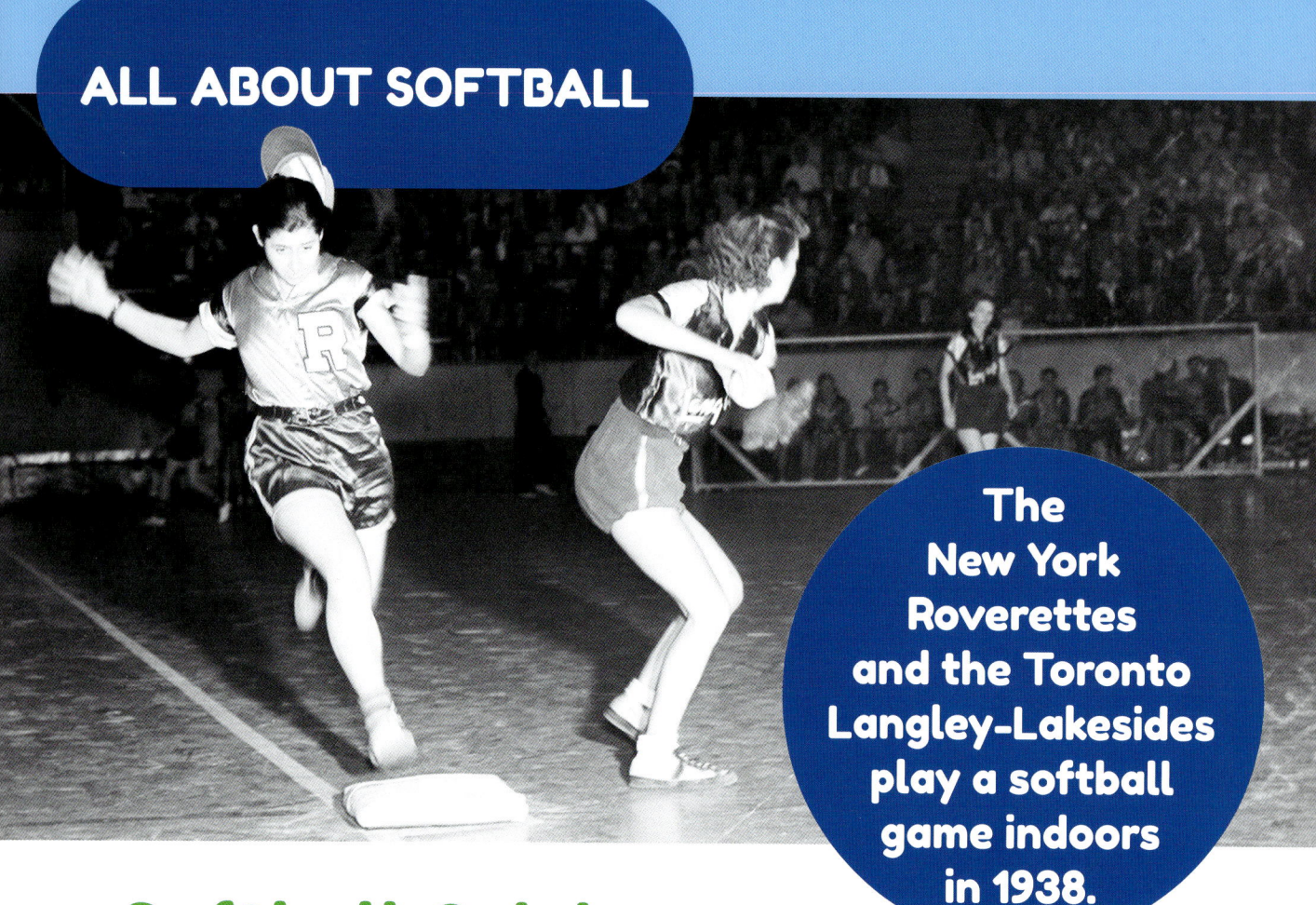

The New York Roverettes and the Toronto Langley-Lakesides play a softball game indoors in 1938.

Softball Origins

Softball was created in the late 1800s. It began as an alternative to baseball to be played indoors. In 1887, the first softball game was played in Chicago. Soon the game began to spread throughout the country. Early names for the sport included "kitten ball" and "pumpkin ball." The name "softball" was adopted in 1926. Standard rules were first published in 1934.

At first the only version of softball was what is now called "slow-pitch." In slow-pitch softball, the pitcher lobs the ball toward the hitter. Fast-pitch softball became popular in the 1930s and 1940s. Fast-pitch was a quicker, more exciting game. It became the main type of softball at competitive levels. It is now played at the college level and internationally.

Marines play softball on a military base in the 1940s.

ALL ABOUT SOFTBALL

Professional Softball

It took years for men's baseball leagues to build their traditions and rivalries. Professional women's softball got a much later start. The first professional women's league came in 1976. That league did not last. Other leagues also came and went.

Women's Professional Baseball

The All-American Girls Professional Baseball League was started in 1943. The league featured teams in Illinois, Indiana, Michigan, Minnesota, and Wisconsin. The league ran for 11 years before folding in 1954.

In 1997, National Pro Fastpitch (NPF) debuted. It folded in 2001 but came back in 2004. For the next 16 years, the league had four to seven teams located around the country. NPF folded in 2021. It was replaced by Athletes Unlimited (AU), which had started in 2020. AU also signed a TV deal with ESPN. A separate league, Women's Professional Fastpitch, started playing in 2022. Despite many stops and starts, women continue to fight for more chances to play professional softball.

Danielle O'Toole delivers a pitch during an Athletes Unlimited softball game in 2020.

ALL ABOUT SOFTBALL

International Softball

Women's fast-pitch softball was added to the Olympics for the 1996 Games in Atlanta. The sport proved popular, especially among the home fans. Team USA won every gold medal until the 2008 Games in Beijing, China. Japan upset Team USA for the gold that year.

Both softball and baseball were dropped as Olympic sports after the 2008 Games. They returned in 2021, when the games were held in Tokyo, Japan. Both sports are popular there. But as of 2022, no plans had been made to continue with either sport at the Olympic level.

International softball continues on, though. National teams from around the world still play tournaments. The Women's Softball World Cup is held every four years. Smaller tournaments are held more often.

Japan celebrates its gold-medal victory at the 2021 Olympics in Tokyo.

ALL ABOUT SOFTBALL

A youth softball catcher chases down a ball in the dirt.

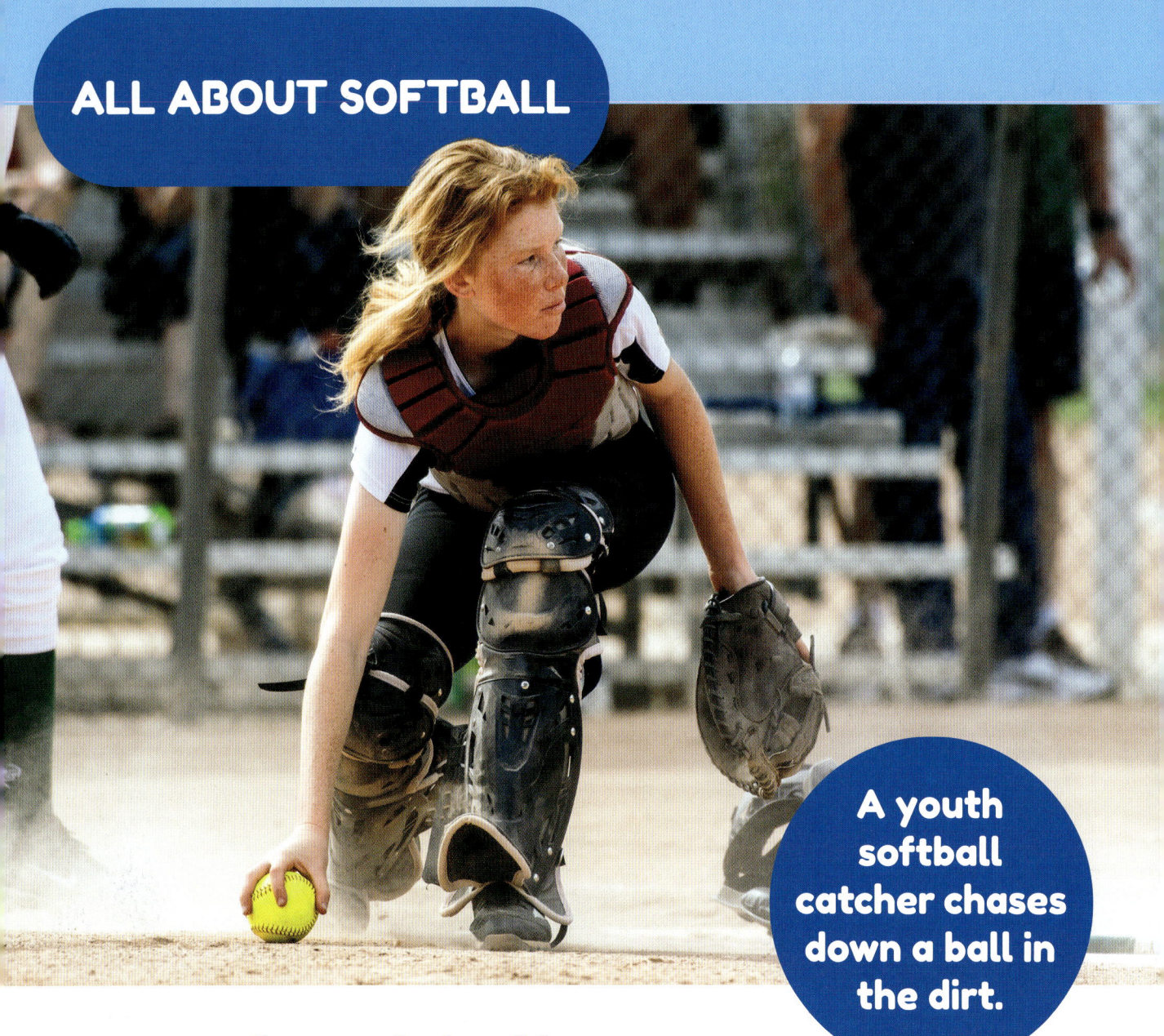

Youth Softball

Fast-pitch softball has long been a popular sport on the youth level. Little League Softball was formed in 1974. It offers leagues for girls ages four to 16. Today, more than 300,000 girls in more than 25 countries play Little League Softball. Like baseball, Little League Softball has its own annual World Series. It is held every August in Greenville, North Carolina.

Many Little League Softball players go on to play high school softball. As of 2019, roughly 362,000 girls played high school softball in the United States. That made it one of the top girls' sports in the country.

> The high school softball season is usually in the spring. But some US states play the sport during the fall.

ALL ABOUT SOFTBALL

College Softball

The National Collegiate Athletic Association (NCAA) began allowing softball in 1910. The college game has only grown from there. In fact, college softball might be the most popular version of the sport. The NCAA has said softball is its fastest growing sport.

A total of 286 schools played Division I college softball during the 2022 season.

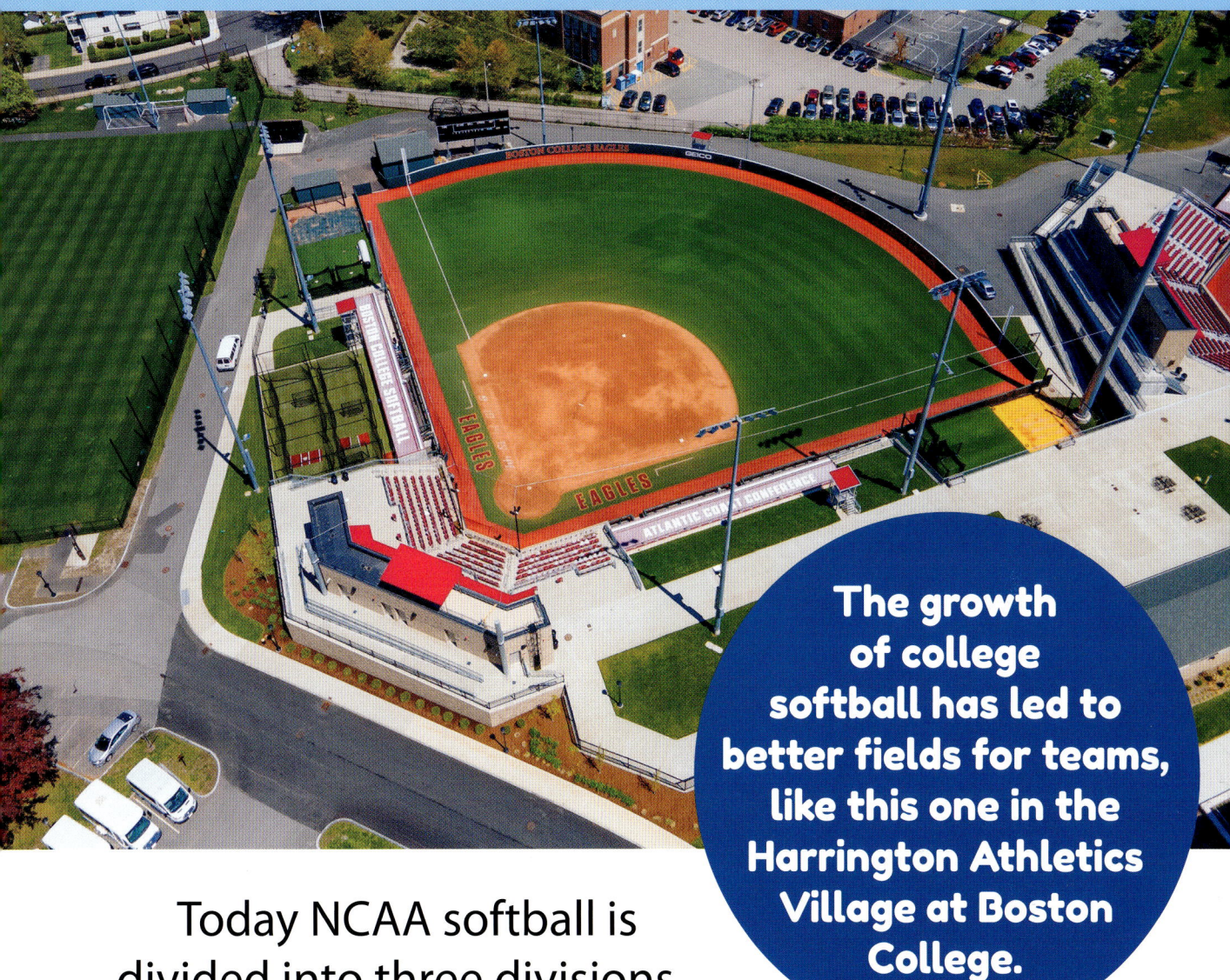

The growth of college softball has led to better fields for teams, like this one in the Harrington Athletics Village at Boston College.

Today NCAA softball is divided into three divisions. The most competitive teams play in Division I. These players are able to earn scholarships to help pay for school. The biggest college softball teams play in front of large crowds and TV audiences.

85

ALL ABOUT SOFTBALL

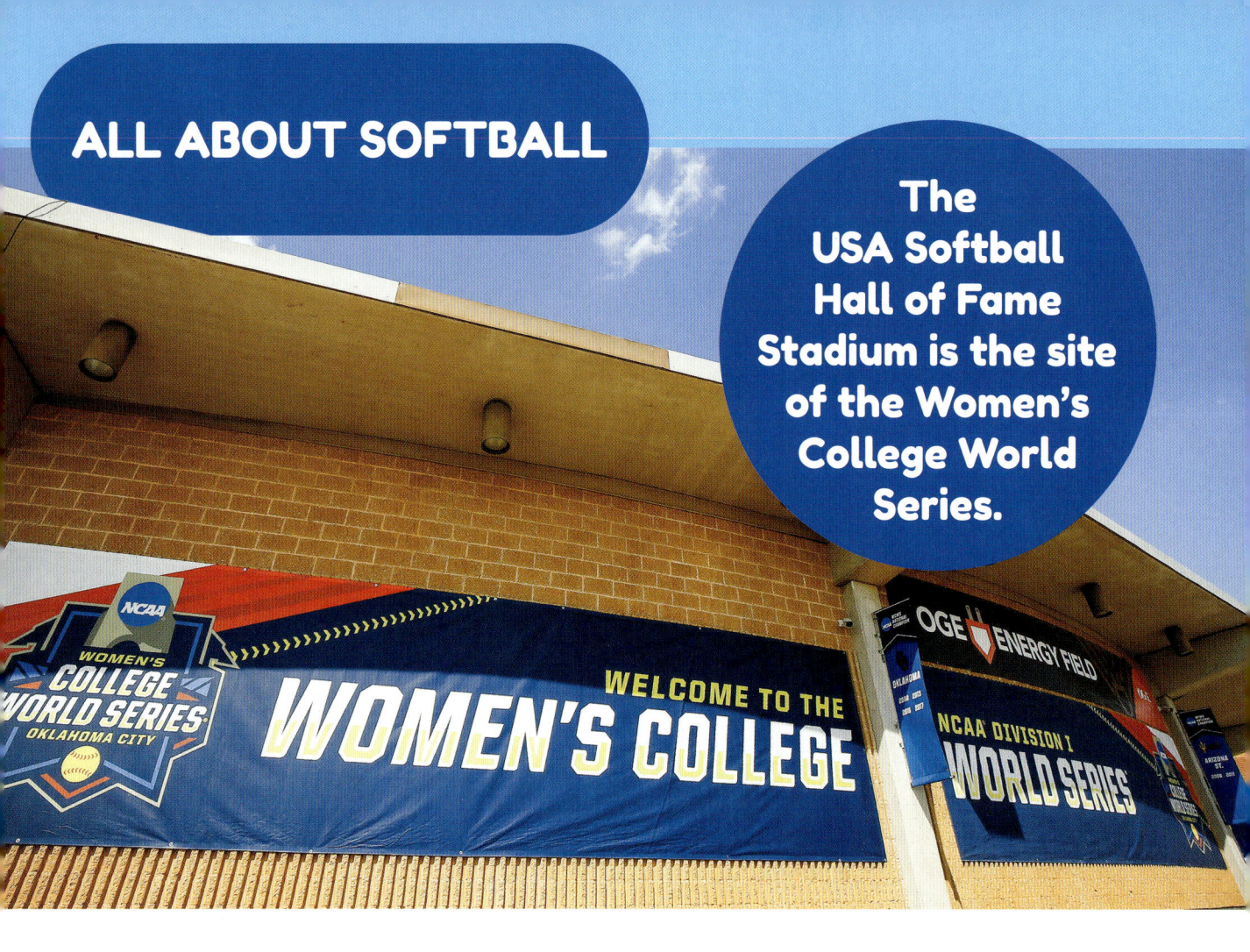

The USA Softball Hall of Fame Stadium is the site of the Women's College World Series.

College Softball World Series

The goal for any Division I softball team is to reach the Women's College World Series (WCWS). The event was first held in 1969. It has served as the NCAA championship since 1982. The WCWS has been held in different locations over the years. Now it takes place every June in Oklahoma City, Oklahoma.

The NCAA Tournament begins with the 64 best teams from the regular season. The final eight teams advance to the WCWS. Once two teams remain, they face off in a best-of-three series to decide the champion.

The WCWS has become more popular. Television ratings have matched those for college baseball. In 2021, the WCWS games averaged more than one million viewers.

UCLA's 12 championships are the most in WCWS history.

TOP BASEBALL TEAMS

New York Yankees

The New York Yankees are the most successful team in MLB history. They began playing in 1903. At the time, they were known as the New York Highlanders. After ten seasons, they changed their name to the Yankees. They won their first World Series in 1923. In 2009, they won their 27th championship. No other team comes close to matching that total.

Joe DiMaggio, *left*, and Mickey Mantle, *right*, are two great players who have worn the Yankees' uniform over the years.

Some of baseball's greatest players became stars with the Yankees. Babe Ruth, Lou Gehrig, Joe DiMaggio, Mickey Mantle, and Derek Jeter all wore the team's navy blue pinstripes. The Yankees won a record five straight World Series from 1949 to 1953. They won four between 1996 and 2000. Today, the team's famous hats can be seen all over the world.

Star shortstop Derek Jeter helped the Yankees win five World Series titles in the 1990s and 2000s.

TOP BASEBALL TEAMS

Catcher Roy Campanella, *center*, hugs pitcher Johnny Podres after the Brooklyn Dodgers won the 1955 World Series.

Los Angeles Dodgers

The Dodgers have a colorful history. They began playing in 1884 in Brooklyn, New York. Over the years, they were known by many nicknames, including the Bridegrooms, Superbas, and Robins. The "Dodgers" nickname finally stuck in 1932. It is a shortened version of "Trolley Dodgers." That was a name for fans who had to avoid the many trolleys on the streets of Brooklyn.

The Dodgers won the World Series only once in Brooklyn, in 1955. Three years later, the team moved to Los Angeles. At the time, they were one of the first teams to play on the West Coast. The Dodgers have added six more championships in Los Angeles.

No. 42
MLB retired jersey No. 42 throughout the league on April 15, 1997, to honor former Dodgers second baseman Jackie Robinson. He wore No. 42 when he broke the MLB color barrier 50 years earlier.

Dodger Stadium was built in 1962.

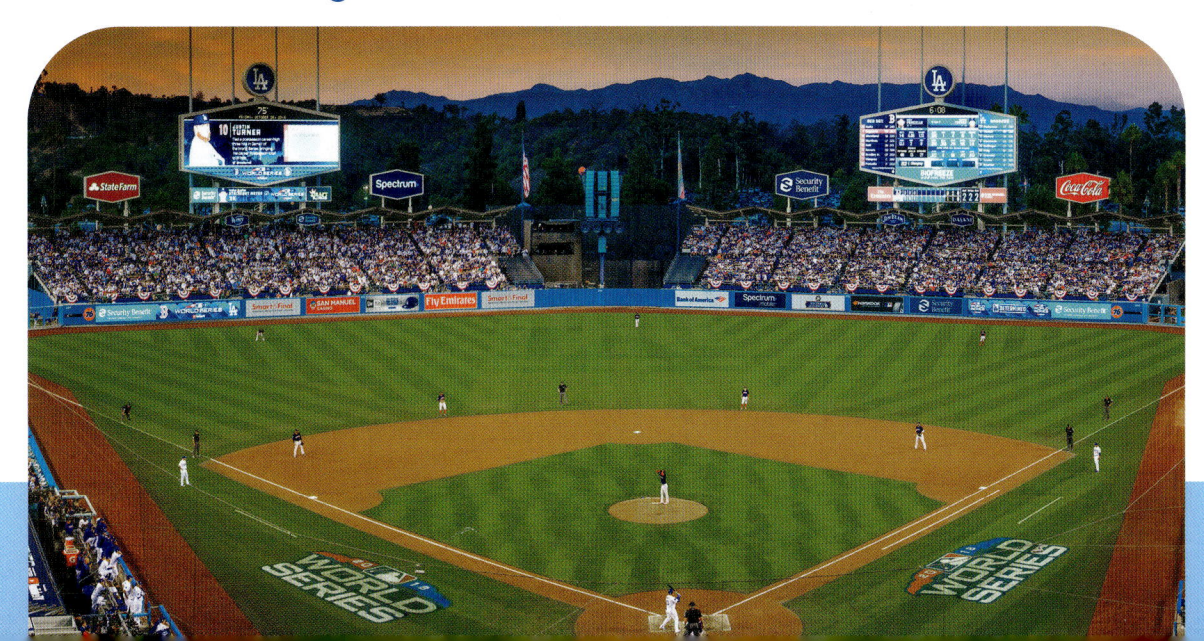

TOP BASEBALL TEAMS

Boston Red Sox

The Boston Americans were one of the first members of the AL in 1901. By 1908, they were known as the Red Sox. And by 1918, they'd won five World Series. But the next year, they made a move that many said

The Comeback

The Boston Red Sox lost the first three games of the 2004 AL Championship Series to the New York Yankees. The Red Sox then won four straight. No other baseball team has ever come back from behind 3–0 to win a playoff series.

The Red Sox jump on closer Keith Foulke after the final out of the 2004 World Series. This was Boston's first championship since 1918.

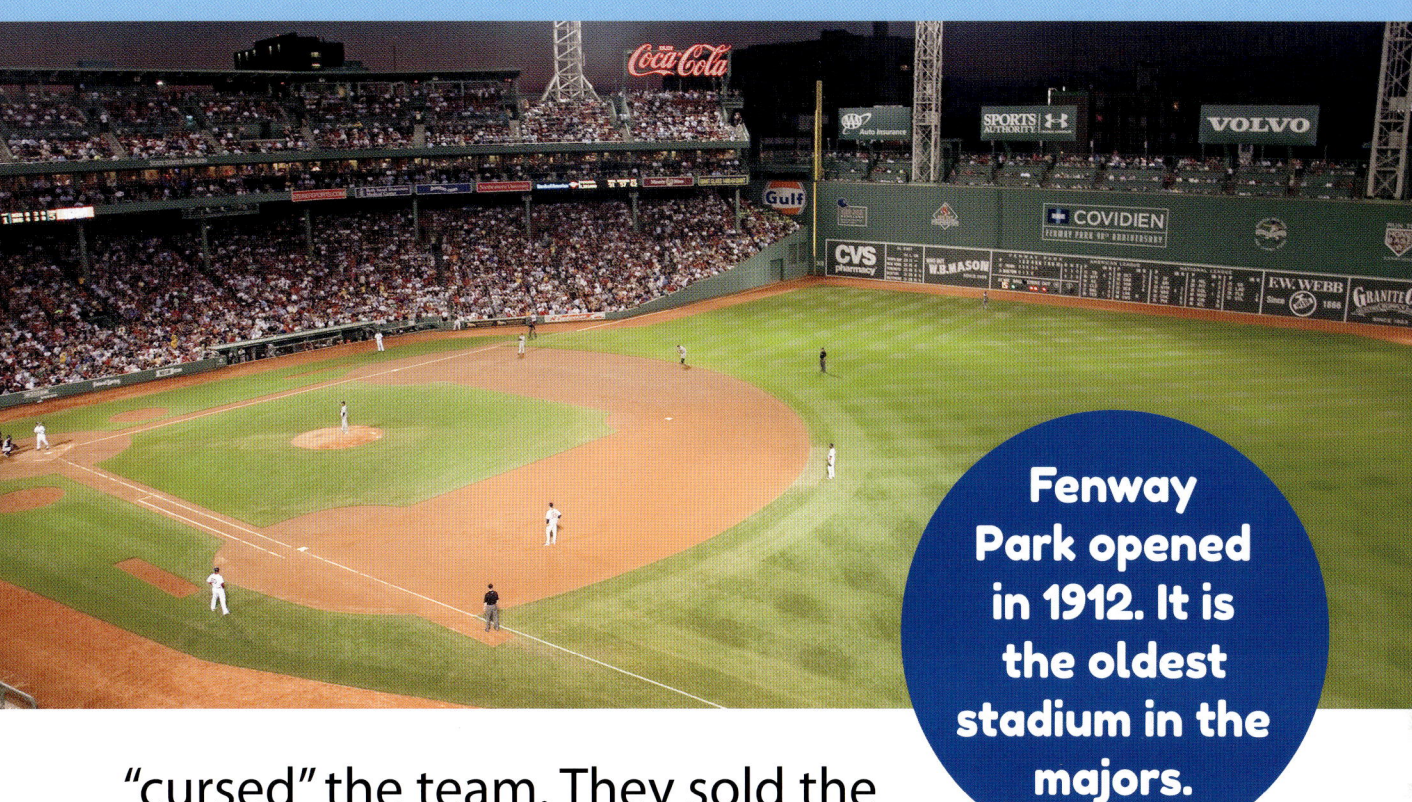

> Fenway Park opened in 1912. It is the oldest stadium in the majors.

"cursed" the team. They sold the contract of a young slugger named Babe Ruth to the New York Yankees. Over the next 86 seasons, they reached the World Series only four times. Each time they lost.

The 2004 Red Sox finally broke the curse. They swept the St. Louis Cardinals for their first title since 1918. Boston added three more World Series championships in 2007, 2013, and 2018. All of that happened while Boston played in the team's legendary home stadium, Fenway Park.

TOP BASEBALL TEAMS

Stan "the Man" Musial helped the Cardinals win three World Series titles in the 1940s.

St. Louis Cardinals

The Cardinals trace their roots to 1882. They were called the Browns for much of their early years. Since 1900, the team has used Cardinals as a nickname.

No NL team has won more World Series than the Cardinals. Their title in 2011 was their 11th.

Many of those wins came from memorable teams. The scrappy "Gashouse Gang" won the 1934 World Series. Superstar slugger Stan Musial led the team to three championships between 1942 and 1946. And ace right-hander Bob Gibson pitched them to titles in 1964 and 1967.

Albert Pujols, one of the greatest hitters of all time, helped the Cardinals win the World Series in 2006 and 2011. More than 3 million fans show up at Busch Stadium every year to cheer on the popular team.

Albert Pujols retired in 2022. He had 3,384 hits and 703 home runs.

TOP BASEBALL TEAMS

Chicago Cubs

Millions of fans have rooted for the Chicago Cubs at the famous Wrigley Field. And while they haven't often been successful, the Cubs have always been beloved.

An NL team has been playing in Chicago since 1876. They've been known as the White Stockings, Colts, and Orphans. They settled on Cubs in 1903. They won four pennants and two World Series between 1906 and 1910.

Wrigley Field has ivy on its outfield wall. The stadium has been the Cubs' home since 1916.

Cubs third baseman Kris Bryant throws his arms up after recording the final out of the 2016 World Series. It was Chicago's first win in 108 years.

Chicago went 0–7 in the World Series between 1910 and 1945. In the years after that, the Cubs then became known as "lovable losers." They rarely made the playoffs. Chicago didn't get back to the World Series until 2016. But that team beat Cleveland in seven games to finally win the title again.

FUN FACT!

Wrigley Field was the last MLB park to install lights. The Cubs played only day games at home until 1988.

TOP BASEBALL TEAMS

John McGraw managed the Giants from 1902 to 1932.

San Francisco Giants

The New York Giants were one of the early powers of the NL. They won ten pennants and three World Series between 1904 and 1924 under legendary manager John McGraw.

Giants slugger Bobby Thomson hit one of the most memorable home runs in history in 1951. His "Shot Heard 'round the World" beat the Dodgers to give the Giants the pennant. Three years later, the electric Willie Mays made one of the most famous catches in history to help the Giants beat Cleveland in the World Series.

The team moved to California in 1958. It took a while to start winning on the West Coast. The Giants finally won again in 2010. They added two more titles in 2012 and 2014.

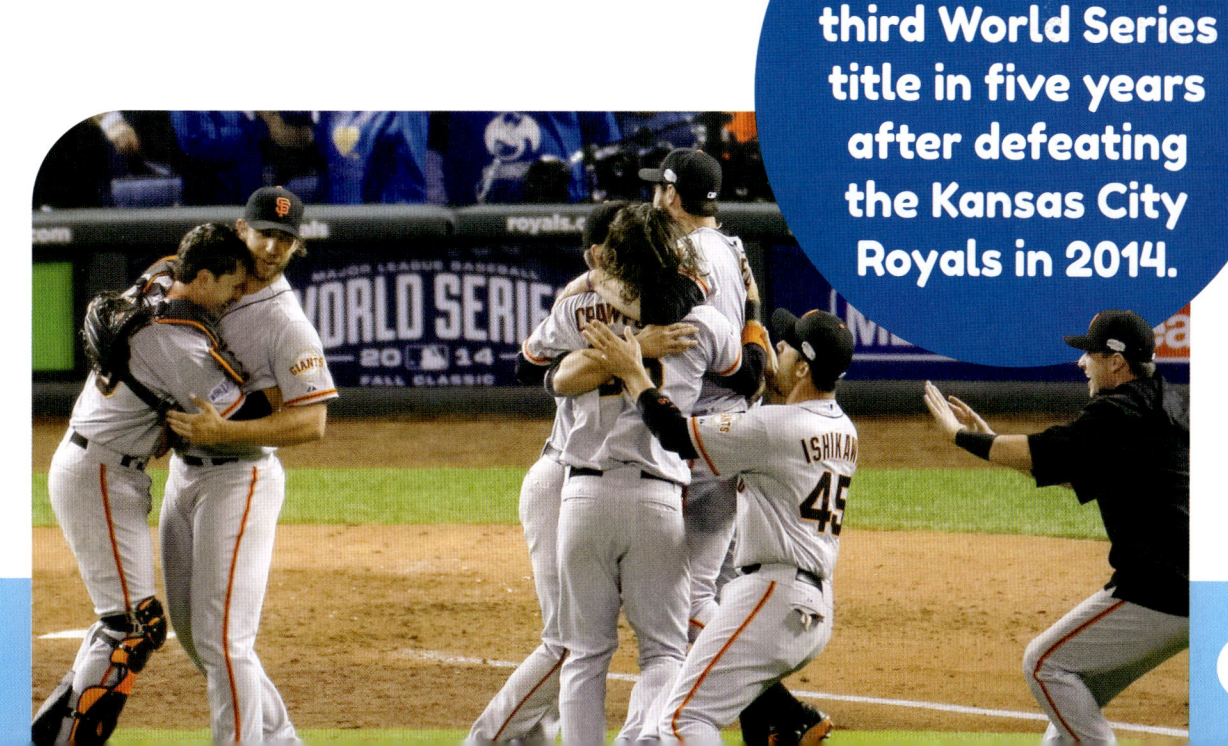

The Giants celebrate their third World Series title in five years after defeating the Kansas City Royals in 2014.

TOP SOFTBALL TEAMS

Team USA

The United States first put together a women's national softball team in 1965. In the years since, it has been the most successful team in the world. Team USA is one of the most popular softball teams in the world, too, along with Japan.

As a national team, Team USA includes only players from the United States. They compete at international tournaments, such as the World Championships. In 1996, softball was added to the Olympics. Team USA won gold that year, and in 2000 and 2004 too. It won silver medals in 2008 and 2021.

Aces of Athens

Team USA went 53–0 in a tour ahead of the 2004 Olympics. Then they won nine games in Athens, Greece, to claim the gold medal.

Team USA celebrates after winning its third straight Olympic gold medal at the 2004 Games in Athens, Greece.

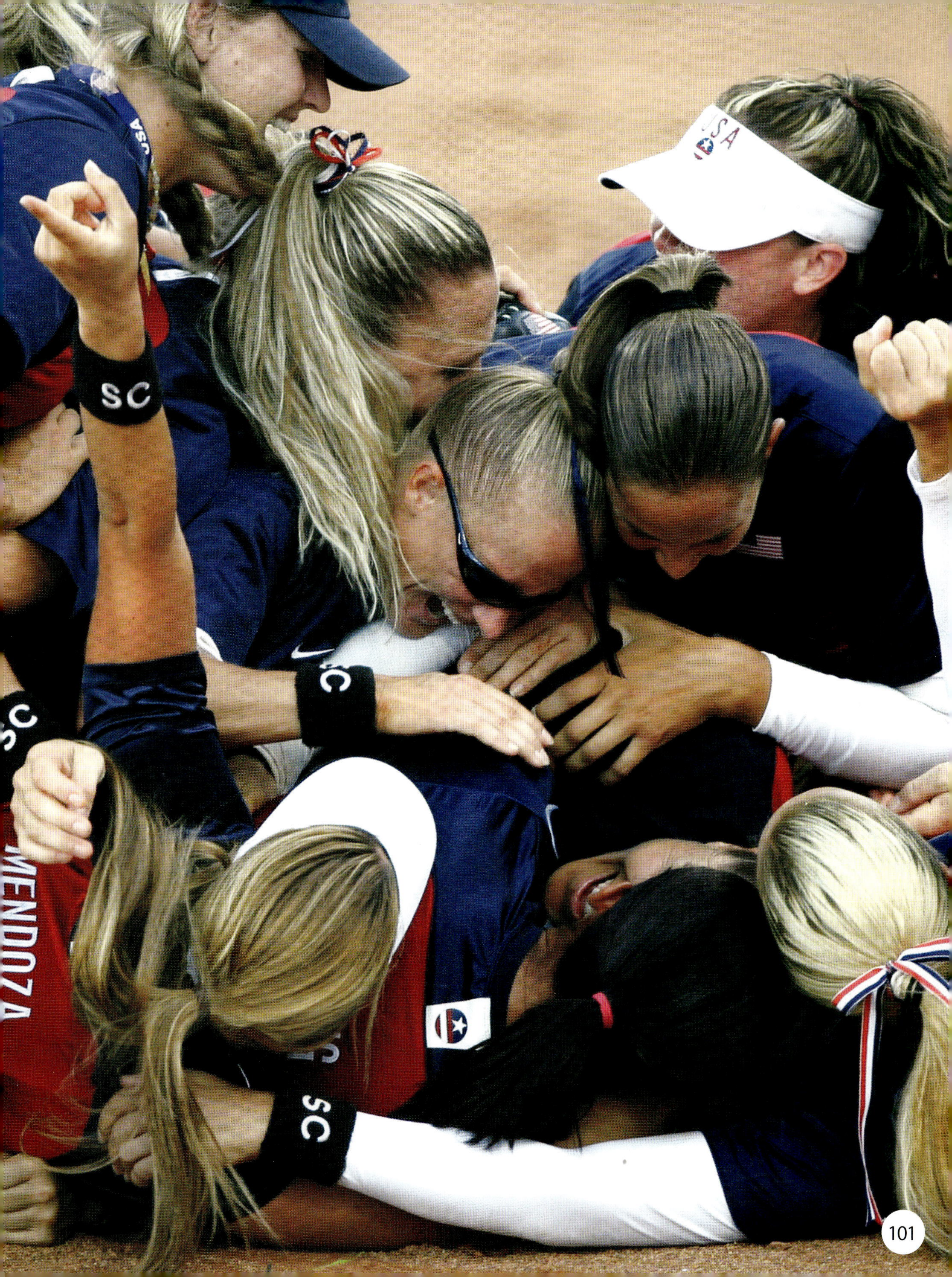
USA
SC
SC
SC
SC
MENDOZA
SC

TOP SOFTBALL TEAMS

University of Arizona

The University of Arizona dominated college softball in the 1990s. The Wildcats won the WCWS in 1991, 1993, 1994, 1996, and 1997. They also finished runner-up three times. The team was led by head coach Mike Candrea. He took over in 1986. When he retired in 2021, Candrea's 1,674 wins were a record.

University of Arizona head coach Mike Candrea, *left*, congratulates Wildcats outfielder Ashleigh Hughes after a home run against UCLA in 2018.

Outfielder Caitlin Lowe, *center,* **celebrates with teammates after scoring the winning run in a 2006 WCWS game.**

One of Candrea's top stars was pitcher Jennie Finch. The right-hander threw eight no-hitters between 1999 and 2002. She also led the Wildcats to another national championship in 2001.

Outfielder Caitlin Lowe was a four-time All-American for Arizona between 2004 and 2007. When Candrea retired, Lowe took over as the school's head coach.

TOP SOFTBALL TEAMS

Head coach Patty Gasso, *right*, turned the Sooners into a powerful team after taking over in 1995.

University of Oklahoma

From 1982 to 2013, the Oklahoma Sooners won only one national title. From 2013 to 2022, Oklahoma added five more. The Sooners also finished runner-up twice in that stretch.

Legendary head coach Patty Gasso has led the Sooners since 1995. In that time, she has won more than 80 percent of her games. Having stars like sluggers like Lauren Chamberlain and later Jocelyn Alo has helped. Chamberlain was the team's main star in 2013. Alo left Oklahoma in 2022 as the nation's all-time leader in home runs. In her senior year, the Sooners finished 59–3. That included a record 38–0 start to the season.

Oklahoma players pile on each other to celebrate winning the 2022 WCWS title.

TOP SOFTBALL TEAMS

UCLA

No team has won more WCWS titles than UCLA. The Bruins won their 12th championship in 2019. One of the biggest reasons was superstar Rachel Garcia. She won her second straight National Player of the Year award that season. Garcia won 29 games as a pitcher. She also hit 11 home runs.

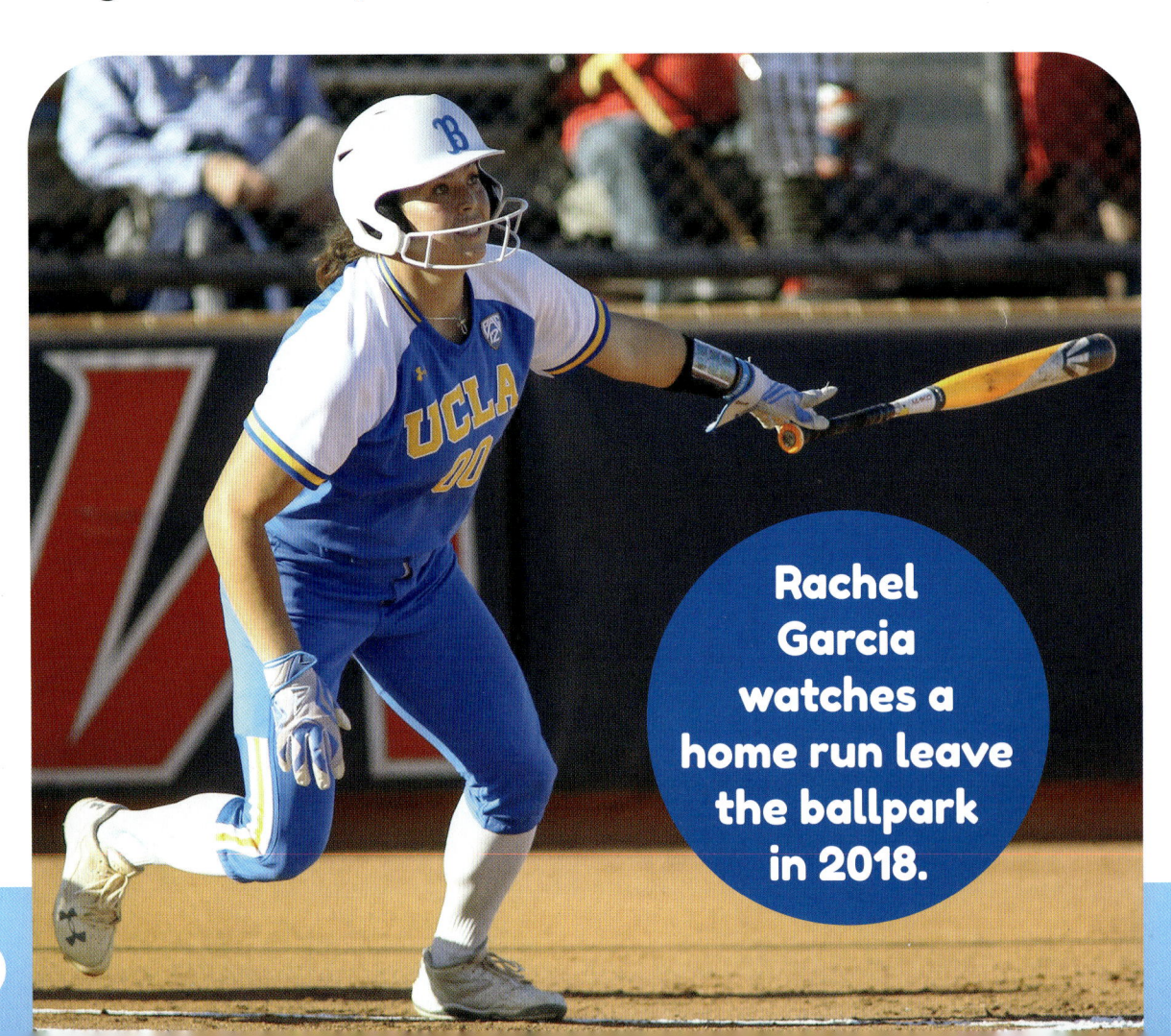

Rachel Garcia watches a home run leave the ballpark in 2018.

UCLA was the sport's first powerhouse team. They won the first WCWS in 1982. They won again in 1984, 1985, and 1988.

The Bruins have had only three head coaches since the program started in 1975. Sharron Backus started the team. She shared the head coaching job with Sue Enquist from 1989 to 1996. The pair won three national titles together. Former star catcher Kelly Inouye-Perez took over for Enquist in 2007.

UCLA's Megan Faraimo delivers a pitch during the 2022 WCWS.

BASEBALL ICONS

Walter Johnson

From 1907 to 1927, Walter Johnson's fastball was the best in baseball. His power pitching earned him the nickname "Big Train." The Washington Senators' star won at least 20 games every year from 1910 to 1919. And his 417 victories are the second most in MLB history.

Sandy Koufax

Sandy Koufax was nearly unhittable for six years from 1961 to 1966. The Los Angeles Dodgers'

Sandy Koufax won the NL Cy Young Award in 1963, 1965, and 1966.

> Mariano Rivera helped the Yankees win five World Series between 1996 and 2009.

lefty won 129 games. He also had an earned-run average (ERA) of just 2.19. The quiet star threw four no-hitters before retiring at age 30 due to arm problems.

Mariano Rivera

Between 1995 and 2013, Mariano Rivera saved a record 652 games for the New York Yankees. The closer featured a dominant pitch called a cut fastball. It would move away from righties and into lefties. Everyone struggled to hit it.

BASEBALL ICONS

Josh Gibson hit .466 while playing for the Homestead Grays in 1943.

Josh Gibson

Josh Gibson is considered the best power hitter in the history of the Negro Leagues. He once hit a 580-foot home run at Yankee Stadium. Historians think he could have broken MLB home run records. But due to segregation, Gibson never got the chance to play in the league.

Johnny Bench

Johnny Bench's defensive skills were flawless. Bench could do it all—block low pitches, throw out would-be base stealers, and call the right pitch at the right time. He also led the NL in home runs twice. Bench was the backbone of Cincinnati's outstanding "Big Red Machine" teams of the 1970s.

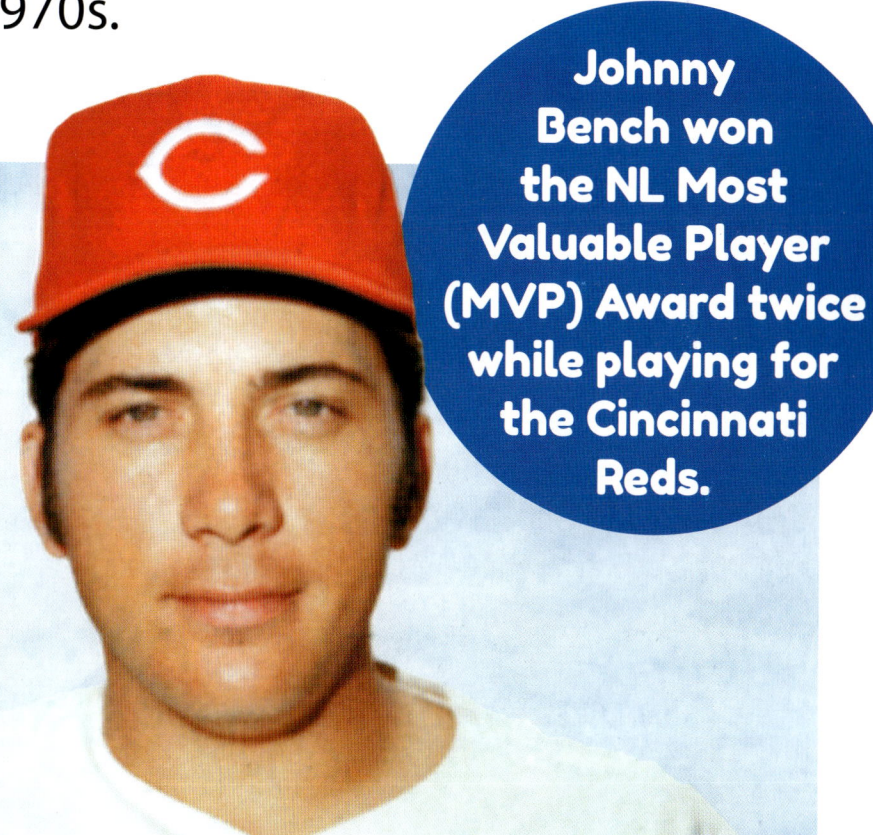

Johnny Bench won the NL Most Valuable Player (MVP) Award twice while playing for the Cincinnati Reds.

BASEBALL ICONS

Lou Gehrig

From 1925 to 1939, Lou Gehrig played every game for the New York Yankees. The "Iron Horse" was a line-drive hitter who also led the league in homers three times. His 185 runs batted in (RBIs) in 1931 set an AL record. He also hit .361 with ten home runs in 34 World Series games. Sadly, an illness cut Gehrig's career and his life short.

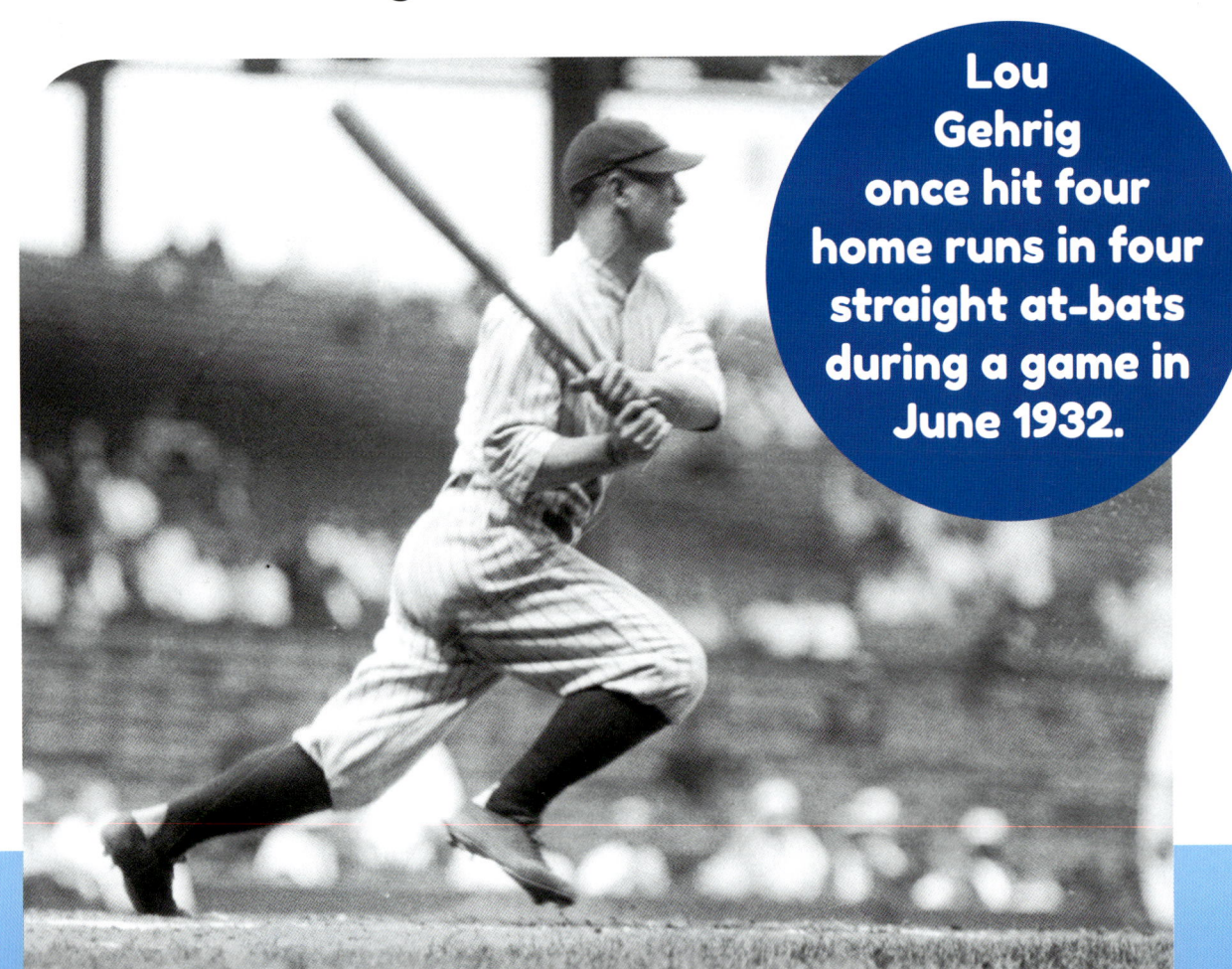

Lou Gehrig once hit four home runs in four straight at-bats during a game in June 1932.

> Jackie Robinson was the first Rookie of the Year Award winner in MLB. The award is now named after him.

Jackie Robinson

Jackie Robinson is best remembered for breaking the MLB color barrier in 1947. He was also one of baseball's toughest competitors. Robinson won the NL MVP Award in his third season. The Brooklyn Dodgers won six pennants and one World Series in Robinson's ten years with the team. His courage and class changed the face of baseball.

BASEBALL ICONS

Cal Ripken Jr.

Baltimore Orioles star Cal Ripken Jr. replaced Lou Gehrig as baseball's Iron Man. Ripken played in a record 2,632 straight games. Along the way, the two-time MVP changed the shortstop position. He was tall and strong but still agile enough to cover plenty of ground in the field. At the plate, Ripken averaged 25 homers and 92 RBIs between 1982 and 1993.

Cal Ripken Jr. waves to the crowd in Baltimore after breaking Lou Gehrig's record in September 1995.

Brooks Robinson

Baltimore Orioles third baseman Brooks Robinson was known for his amazing fielding. He won 16 straight Gold Glove Awards from 1960 to 1975. Robinson is best remembered for his performance in the 1970 World Series. He hit .429 with two homers to win the series MVP award. He also made several standout fielding plays to steal hits from Cincinnati Reds batters.

Brooks Robinson was known as "the Human Vacuum Cleaner" for his amazing fielding.

BASEBALL ICONS

Ted Williams hit .344 in his career.

Ted Williams

Ted Williams had one of the sweetest swings ever. "The Splendid Splinter" is the last man to hit .400, hitting .406 in 1941. He also won the AL Triple Crown in 1942 and 1947. Williams missed three seasons while serving in the military. But he still hit 521 career home runs.

Willie Mays

Willie Mays was a hero to many fans from the early 1950s to the mid-1970s. Over the course of his career, Mays won four home run titles and four stolen base titles. The "Say Hey Kid" also played center field with flair for the New York/San Francisco Giants and New York Mets.

Barry Bonds

Barry Bonds won seven MVP Awards between 1986 and 2007. The San Francisco Giants and Pittsburgh Pirates star also retired with a record 762 career homers. But rumors that he used performance-enhancing drugs have damaged his legacy.

FUN FACT!

One of Willie Mays's teammates was Bobby Bonds, Barry's father. Mays is Barry Bonds's godfather.

Barry Bonds, *left*, and Willie Mays, *right*, both starred for the Giants.

BASEBALL ICONS

Babe Ruth

Babe Ruth led the majors in home runs 11 times. In 1927, the "Bambino" hit 60, a record that stood for 34 years. And the New York Yankee's larger-than-life personality made him one of the most famous people in the world.

FUN FACT! When Babe Ruth hit 54 homers in 1920, it was more than any other AL team had hit all season.

New York's Yankee Stadium became known as the "House that Ruth Built" because Babe Ruth hit so many home runs there.

Hank Aaron watches a home run leave the park during a game in the early 1970s.

Hank Aaron

Hank Aaron broke Ruth's career record for home runs in 1974. He did it by being consistent. Aaron never hit more than 50 home runs in any season for the Milwaukee/Atlanta Braves and Milwaukee Brewers. But he averaged 37 homers from 1955 to 1973.

Mike Trout

The powerful, speedy Mike Trout was the best player of the 2010s. In his first nine seasons, he won three AL MVP Awards. In 2022, he hit 40 homers for the third time in his career.

SOFTBALL ICONS

Cat Osterman

Cat Osterman pitched in three Olympic Games. The left-hander helped the team win gold in 2004 and silver in 2008. In 2021, the 38-year-old helped the US team won another silver medal. In her career with Team USA, Osterman was 74–5 with a 0.44 ERA. And she struck out 1,030 batters in 519 innings pitched.

Cat Osterman was named one of the top college softball pitchers of all time by a 2022 article.

Lisa Fernandez won Olympic medals with Team USA in 1996, 2000, and 2004.

Lisa Fernandez

Lisa Fernandez was a star pitcher and hitter. The Californian led the US team to three straight Olympic gold medals starting in 1996. She went 7–1 with an ERA of 0.36 in those three Games. She also hit .302 with 15 RBIs. Fernandez set an Olympic record with 25 strikeouts in a game in 2000. And she hit .545 to lead the United States to its last gold medal in 2004.

FUN FACT!

Jennie Finch was another huge part of the 2004 Olympic team. Finch went 2–0 at the Games. In eight innings pitched, she allowed only one hit. Finch also struck out 13 batters.

SOFTBALL ICONS

Dot Richardson celebrates scoring a run against Puerto Rico at the 1996 Olympics in Atlanta.

Dot Richardson

Dot Richardson was a hard-hitting shortstop who was a big success on and off the field. She was a four-time college All-American in the 1980s. Then she took a break from studying to be a doctor as softball made its Olympic debut in 1996. Richardson's two-run homer clinched the gold medal for Team USA.

Yukiko Ueno

Japan broke Team USA's hold on the Olympic gold medal in 2008. Yukiko Ueno was the team's biggest star. The right-handed pitcher threw 21 innings in one day to get her team to the gold-medal game. Then she pitched a complete game in the final. In 2021, Ueno helped Japan win a second gold medal.

Yukiko Ueno delivers a pitch during the 2021 Olympics in Tokyo.

SOFTBALL ICONS

Haylie McCleney

Haylie McCleney is known for making diving catches and smashing into walls to take away home runs. She was a four-time All-American at the University of Alabama. And she was one of Team USA's stars at the Tokyo Olympics in 2021. She led the Americans with a .529 batting average and nine hits as they won a silver medal.

Haylie McCleney makes a diving catch while playing for Alabama in 2014.

Jocelyn Alo hits a home run in the 2021 WCWS Final against Florida State University.

Jocelyn Alo

No power hitter had a better college career than Jocelyn Alo at Oklahoma. On March 11, 2022, Alo hit her 96th career home run. That broke the NCAA record. Alo finished her career with 122 long balls. She is also the only college player to hit 30 or more home runs in three different seasons.

FUN FACT!

The home run record broken by Jocelyn Alo was held by Lauren Chamberlain. Like Alo, Chamberlain also played at Oklahoma. Chamberlain graduated in 2015.

GLOSSARY

carbon fiber
A strong material used to make baseball and softball bats.

compete
To engage in a sport against an opponent.

competitive
Equally matched to an opposing team or athlete.

competitors
Individuals or teams opposing each other in a sporting event.

count
The number of balls and strikes on a batter during an at-bat.

desegregate
To undo the practice of separating groups of people based on race, gender, ethnicity, or other factors.

infield
The dirt cutout of a baseball field that contains the pitcher's mound and all four bases.

myth
A popular story that is not true.

outfield
The grass part of a field between the infield and the fence.

pennant
Another name for a league championship; in MLB, it refers to winning either the American or National League championship.

pinstripes
Thin vertical stripes seen on clothing.

segregation
The act of keeping people or things apart.

TO LEARN MORE

More Books to Read

Abdo, Kenny. *History of Baseball*. Abdo, 2020.

Abdo, Kenny. *Miracle Moments in Baseball*. Abdo, 2022.

Flynn, Brendan. *Girls' Softball*. Abdo, 2022.

Online Resources

Booklinks
NONFICTION NETWORK
FREE! ONLINE NONFICTION RESOURCES

To learn more about baseball and softball, please visit **abdobooklinks.com** or scan this QR code. These links are routinely monitored and updated to provide the most current information available.

INDEX

Major League Baseball (MLB), 4, 40, 46, 52, 57, 60, 62–63, 64–65, 66, 70–71, 72, 74, 88, 91, 97, 108, 110, 113

Negro Leagues, 62–63, 110

Women's College World Series (WCWS), 86–87, 102, 106–107

World Series, 4, 61, 72, 74–75, 88–89, 91, 92–93, 94–95, 96–97, 98–99, 112–113, 115

PHOTO CREDITS

Cover Photos: Shutterstock Images, front (left), back (baseball); Sarah Stier/Getty Images Sport/Getty Images, front (middle); Jon Osumi/Shutterstock Images, front (right); Chris Hill/Shutterstock Images, front (background); Tammy Kay Photo/Shutterstock Images, back (pitcher)

Interior Photos: Bill Florence/Shutterstock Images, 1, 27, 41; Shutterstock Images, 3, 8, 55; iStockphoto, 4, 6, 14 (left), 25, 59; Brian Bahr/Getty Images Sport/Getty Images, 5, 45, 87, 105, 107; Jon Osumi/Shutterstock Images, 7, 16, 20, 30, 31, 51, 82; Andy Mead/YCJ/Icon Sportswire/Getty Images, 9; Koji Watanabe/Getty Images Sport/Getty Images, 11 (top); Tammy Kay Photo/Shutterstock Images, 11 (bottom); Romaro Images/Shutterstock Images, 13; Thearon W. Henderson/Getty Images Sport/Getty Images, 14 (right), 29; Alex Gombash/iStockphoto, 15 (top); Tok Anas/Shutterstock Images, 15 (bottom left); Suzanne Tucker/Shutterstock Images, 15 (bottom right); Matt York/AP Images, 18; Melissa Tamez/Image of Sport/AP Images, 19; Clive Rose/Getty Images Sport/Getty Images, 21; Mykhallo Bokovan/Shutterstock Images, 23 (field); Arna Photo/Shutterstock Images, 23 (jerseys); Sarah Stier/Getty Images Sport/Getty Images, 24, 125; Debby Wong/Shutterstock Images, 26, 89, 109; Dennis Poroy/Getty Images Sport/Getty Images, 28; Cynthia Farmer/Shutterstock Images, 33; Colin E. Braley, 34–35; Jan de Wild/Shutterstock Images, 36; Alika Jenner/Getty Images Sport/Getty Images, 37; Jon Ewing/Portland Press Herald/Getty Images, 38; Rich Graessle/Icon Sportswire/Getty Images, 39; C. Morgan Engel/NCAA Photos/Getty Images, 40; Rich Graessle/Corbis/Icon Sportswire/Getty Images, 42; Jeff Gritchen/Digital First Media/Orange County Register/MediaNews Group/Getty Images, 43; Gregory Fischer/Icon Sportswire/Getty Images, 44; Jamie Schwaberow/NCAA Photos/Getty Images, 45; Richard Rodriguez/AP Images, 46; Duane Burleson/Getty Images Sport/Getty Images, 47; Kazuhiro Fujihara/AFP/Getty Images, 48; Andy Cross/The Denver Post/Getty Images, 49; Bruce Leighty/Sports Images/Alamy , 50; Beto Chagas/Shutterstock Images, 53; Susan Leggett/Shutterstock Images, 54; Duane Burleson/AP Images, 56; Chad McDermott/Shutterstock Images, 57; Corbis Historical/Getty Images, 58; Mark Rucker/Transcendental Graphics/Getty Images Sport/Getty Images, 60, 110; Bettmann/Getty Images, 61, 76, 88, 112, 116, 118; Matty Zimmerman/AP Images, 62; Sporting News/Getty Images, 63; George Rinhart/Corbis Historical/Getty Images, 64; University of Southern California Libraries/Corbis Historical/Getty Images, 65; Jason Miller/Getty Images Sport/Getty Images, 66; Ariana Cubillos/AP Images, 67; Tom E. Puskar/AP Images, 68; Sean M. Haffey/Getty Images Sport/Getty Images, 69; Mike Janes/Four Seam Images/AP Images, 70; Red Line Editorial, 71, 73; Rob Tringali/MLB Photos/Getty Images, 74; Bill Kostroun/AP Images, 75; Still Media Collection/US Marine Corps Archives and Special Collections, 77; Quinn Harris/Getty Images Sport/Getty Images, 79; Daisuke Tomita/The Yomiuri Shimbun/AP Images, 81; Joe SA Photos/Shutterstock Images, 83; Jacob Snow/Icon Sportswire/Getty Images, 84, 106; Wangkun Jia/Shutterstock Images, 85; Shane Bevel/NCAA Photos/Getty Images, 86; AP Images, 90, 94, 98, 111; Joseph Sohm/Shutterstock Images, 91, 93; Stephen Dunn/Getty Images Sport/Getty Images, 92; Matt Trommer/Shutterstock Images, 95; Steve Broer/Shutterstock Images, 96; Ian Johnson/Icon Sportswire/AP Images, 97; Carlos Avila Gonzalez/The San Francisco Chronicle/Hearst Newspapers/Getty Images, 99; Omar Torres/AFP/Getty Images, 101; Jacob Snow/Icon Sportswire/AP Images, 102; Bryan Terry/The Oklahoman/AP Images, 103; Jerry Laizure/AP Images, 104; Focus on Sport/Getty Images, 108, 115; Photo File/MLB Photos/Hulton Archive/Getty Images, 113; Roberto Borea/AP Images, 114; Jeff Haynes/AFP/Getty Images, 117; Tony Tomsic/AP Images, 119; Sue Ogrocki/AP Images, 120; Eric Gay/AP Images, 121; Joel Robine/AFP/Getty Images, 122; Jae C. Hong/AP Images, 123; Vasha Hunt/AL.com/AP Images, 124